YOUR BEST DECADE

Ryan *B* Fahey

Copyright © 2019 Ryan B Fahey

All rights reserved. No part of this publication may be reproduced, stored in a retrieval system, or transmitted, in any form or in any means – by electronic, mechanical, photocopying, recording or otherwise – without prior written permission.

This book would not have been possible without my loving, supportive wife and my family who helped me get this book into your hands. To everyone who helped me from start to finish, thank you for your love, care, and generosity!

CONTENTS

Introduction: Start With Y 1

Chapter 1: Unlimited Potential 5

Chapter 2: Fully Living With Intention 15

Chapter 3: The Three Truths of Significance 29

Chapter 4: Abundance Thinking 41

Chapter 5: Legacy > Resume 57

Chapter 6: Take Your Temperature 77

Chapter 7: Burn Boats Not Bridges 79

Chapter 8: The Stories We Tell Ourselves 95

Chapter 9: Abandon The Comfort Zone 109

Chapter 10: The Yes/No Equation 123

Chapter 11: The Hungriest Person In The Room 145

Chapter 12: Got It? Give it! 163

Appendix: My Top Ten Book Recommendations 169

INTRODUCTION
Start With Y

> *"Wellness is a series of decisions that take you from living a good life, to living your best life."*

It is 8:12 pm on Saturday, September 9th, 2017 and I am sitting in my hotel room in Abu Dhabi writing this book for you. Who knew I would be twenty eight, living in the UAE with little to no liquid assets to my name, working for a place that virtually does not exist to many people, and still able to write a book to help you live life abundantly, regardless of which decade you find yourself in.

Your best decade (YBD) is about living to your absolute potential in what I call the 'Big Three' areas of your life. More simply, how can you see and live according to your values **professionally, personally** and **relationally** at twenty-eight, thirty-eight or seventy-eight? Living and breathing the big three in your best decade starts with you, your environment and your mindset!

Before diving in, I want to thank my incredible life partner Amber, my parents, and other friends and family members who have helped me get to where I am today by teaching me the power of responsibility, accountability, and integrity. It is through these lessons, and the ability to be a good student, that I have been blessed professionally, personally, and relationally. Leadership is really simple in that if you say you are going to do something, you do it. This is something my father taught me as a young boy and I am truly grateful to have been raised by such amazing parents. Thank you!

Jim Dotson, a wise friend of mine who authored the book titled *Taking On Goliath*, once said, "*I am not an author, but I have a story to tell.*" That is true of this book as well. My story begins somewhere in the traceable steps of a dirt road in rural Nova Scotia.

Growing up in Oxford, Nova Scotia, I never thought I would be where I am today. Life was simple. Go to school. Drink lots of Tim Hortons coffee. Play high school sports. Then work a humble job, which likely started before graduation, so that you could buy yourself a dog and a small car. Oxford is a 'work hard' town that gave me opportunities to grow, become resilient, and learn many lessons about relationships, humility, and integrity. It is more than just the Blueberry Capital of Canada: it is a hidden gem filled with good-hearted people; a modest town; and a nice place to raise a family surrounded by great people whom I am thankful for. There is definitely something to be said about growing up in a small town.

Now, let me give you my first powerful thought: Have humble beginnings. Humility is found within the hearts of many champions and a recorded trait in many documented leaders who are no longer with us. Humility is timeless. Former President Benjamin Franklin was a postman before becoming one of the founding fathers of the United States of America. He would occasionally walk with his head down. As a Postman, he did this because he would always be looking for money. He was noted to say: *"A penny found is a penny earned."* He knew his humble beginnings.

Wherever you end up after reading this book, always keep your time zone set on humility and your compass set to the humble beginnings that raised you to where you are today and to where you will be tomorrow.

My life today is still quite simple, and the way I consistently choose wellness and personal growth leadership is something you need to be ready to consider for your life as well if you are reading this book. You will also have to make time to excavate your own values, project achievable goals, and build strategies to help create the most amazing version of yourself. This book is not glamorous nor is it filled with easy hacks to improve your life, but I guarantee that it will be the best money you spend this month. My goal in writing this book is that you learn some strategies and counsel that will help you create your best decade.

Before we dive in too deep, remember that your best decade is not defined by a number or by a specific date on the calendar. Sorry to disappoint you here. ***Living out your best decade is a journey.*** What I mean is that your best decade is simply living the next ten years of your life in alignment with your values according to your greatest ability through tools that will give birth to the highest quality living experience, which can roll into the following decades of your life. Your best decade is not an end goal, but rather a continuum for blessings professionally, personally and relationally yet to be discovered.

I know that most of you reading this have very large hearts and you want to make a difference in the world. That is probably why you decided to invest in yourself by reading this book. Thank you for deciding to invest in yourself! It is the single greatest investment you can make. By the time this book gets to you I hope to be leagues beyond where I was when I first wrote to you. My goal is that you, too, will be a league beyond your current self once you finish this book. Get ready to dig in, get dirty when you need to get dirty and build a life that will allow you to live on your own terms.

This book will challenge you, push you, and recreate you in many different ways. It will allow you to escape your current circumstances strategically, and *it will give you permission to say no to the wrong things in order to also say yes to the right things.* This book will give you step by step strategies to build a legacy of leadership through personal growth thinking, regardless of the role or chapter of life you find yourself. It will help you create, build and sustain relationships in all areas of your life. It will also allow you to trim your life down to the basics of what drives you to live and allow you to flourish daily from here on out.

Get ready to buckle up for the ride of your life. Your best decade is going to be the best meal you have ever eaten and the step by step recipe is laid out in front of you. It is in your hands. Let the preparation begin!

CHAPTER 1
Unlimited Potential

> *"The will to win, the desire to succeed, the urge to reach your full potential...These are the keys that will unlock the door to personal excellence."*
>
> —Confucius

I WILL NOT WASTE your time sugar coating the pathway that you will take to create your best decade. Creating your best decade is much more than a one size fits all recipe and it is much more than a quick fix. Ten-minute oil changes are great, but ten years of your life at its best takes time. It is a day-to-day grind that begins now.

It is a combination of reading and applying the principles in this chapter, as well as others in this book, to help launch and sustain your best decade. It should not start and stop within the pages of this book, either. It is my aim that the words written within these chapters push you and challenge your way of life in different areas to help you become your best self by living a rich and fulfilling life. Reaching your unlimited potential will require you to think differently and to reallocate your time more effectively. This process can be painful, frustrating, emotional, and overwhelming so buckle up.

If you want to create your best decade, it is time to let go of your ego and allow yourself to get real in all areas of your life. When the student is ready, the lesson reveals itself.

Be the student.

Be ready.

Allow yourself to be your best student through the following chapters of this book.

I wanted to start this book off by getting you to unpack your current potential and determine where you need to improve in order to begin to create your best decade. I recently read an amazing book by John C. Maxwell titled *No Limits*, about blowing the lid off of your capacity. In an effort to build on his leadership, I decided that the best way to start this book is to share with you how you can create unlimited potential within yourself through capacity building. We all possess potential and we all have different areas of capacity which collectively allow us to reach our unlimited potential. We all have between eleven to twelve capacity areas in our lives. This number fluctuates based on the chapter of life and the decade you find yourself in.

Let me articulate this in more detail for you. ***Capacity is the ability to reach your maximum, daily.*** In long distance running, capacity is measured as your lactate threshold, or your ability to run a certain pace over an extended period of time without 'cramping up' or needing to stop to catch your breath from exhaustion. Capacity is just that: a cap. Most people think about a cap as the limit, but those people are not thinking about capacity properly. Instead of a cap on one jar, why not have one thousand jars with caps? Let me explain.

We all have multiple capacities within us. *Relational, professional, and intellectual* are just a few. Let's focus on these three jars of capacities to start.

If I were to evaluate my relational capacity right now, I would say it is about an 8 out of 10. Room for improvement for sure. I can always do more for my partner to serve her. I can meet her needs better and support her more. Ten years from now that may change; that is ok.

My professional capacity was about an 8 out of 10 in 2016/17 while working over fifty hours a week in Alberta, Canada. Currently, my professional capacity is about 9.5 out of 10. Why the change? I can actually accomplish more professionally while working thirty-five to forty-five hours a week at multiple jobs than I could by working over fifty hours a week in one job. Depending on what demands are found in your current job, your numbers may fluctuate as well.

Similarly, my intellectual capacity is also different than it was one, two, and even three years ago. Although I was educated before moving to the UAE, I had a very North American view of the world. Since moving to Abu Dhabi, my intellectual capacity has exploded. Reading books has been a priority, as has conversing with people from across multiple cultures. My newspaper reading is much richer; journaling even more so. My thinking is clearer and my writing and goal-setting are continually evolving as I develop intellectually. This being said, my intellectual capacity is about a 9 out of 10. If, or when, I start my

Masters, it will likely increase to a ten for that chapter of my life. There is much to learn in your best decade.

I share all of this because you can do your own evaluation of these three areas of your capacity as well. Take a moment to think about these three specific areas…..Your relationships, your profession, and your personal intellect. Where do they all rank out of 10? Doing this evaluation in these areas as well as in all areas of your life is the first step to reaching your unlimited potential.

If your areas score lower than a five, it is time to switch gears to better focus on improving that specific area of your capacity. Go easy on yourself here too. Often people tend to be harder on themselves than they should be, so give yourself a fair evaluation. Do not slide into comparative thinking towards someone else's potential either. Focus on your own personal potential and be honest with yourself.

Once you have completed evaluations for these three areas you are ready to evaluate all areas of your capacity out of ten:

Mental Capacity - How am I in my ability to be resilient in my 'big three' areas while also being mindful about my thoughts? How do I think when times are challenging? How am I in this area out of 10?

Score:

Emotional Capacity - How am I able to connect emotionally with myself? With my significant other? With family? Friends? Am I able to love bigger? How am I in this category out of 10?

Score:

Spiritual Capacity - Am I spiritually able to give more than I have been giving? Am I able to love more than I have been loving? How strong are my beliefs out of 10?

Score:

Physical Capacity - Am I able to be physically healthier? Am I moving regularly? Am I able to create space for quality physical activity in my weekly schedule? How am I out of 10 in this area?

Score:

Social Capacity - Do I socialize? Can I socialize more intentionally? What do I like to do socially? (*Big question in your teens, twenties, thirties and beyond*). How am I here out of 10?

Score:

Environmental Capacity - Do I take steps daily to reduce my environmental impact? Am I consciously aware of how my life impacts the environment locally? At-large? How am I in this area out of 10?

Score:

Leadership Capacity - Am I an effective leader in my area of work? Life? How am I able to lead better in all areas of my life? How am I in this area out of 10?

Score:

Creative Capacity - Am I creating the life I want? Am I putting creative thinking into my projects, hobbies, and passions? Could I do more here? How am I in this area out of 10?

Score:

Communication Capacity - Do I communicate effectively with others? With myself? Am I mindful about the way I communicate? Can I communicate through a lens of understanding? How am I in this area out of 10?

Score:

Financial Capacity - Am I being smart with my finances? Can I spend my money more effectively? Am I balancing my giving, spending, and saving? How am I in this category out of 10?

Score:

Intellectual Capacity - Am I challenging my thinking and my intellect on a weekly basis? What am I able to read to push the boundaries of my thinking? How am I in this area out of 10?

Score:

Parental Capacity (*if applicable*) - Am I a good parent? Do I lead by example for my children? Do my words align with my actions daily? How am I doing in this category out of 10?

Score:

You may have found this evaluation challenging and perhaps, it also revealed emotions which lead you to believe you are not doing enough. You are not alone: I feel the same way every single time I do this exercise. That is a good thing! This means you are embedding the idea into your subconscious that you need to become better and greater in certain areas of your life. You are subconsciously setting the bar higher. That in itself represents growth. Growth happens when awareness is gained. This is the exact thinking you need in order to get you living a life of unlimited potential!

There are a total of twelve capacities listed above (*including parental capacity*). Collectively, all of these capacities add up to your overall potential.

If you scored a ten for each category in your personal evaluation you are currently reaching your individual unlimited potential. Your score would be 120. If you did this evaluation honestly, I doubt that you scored 120, and that is completely ok!

If you scored yourself with a 9 in each category your score would be 108. With a score of 108, you may not be fully reaching your capacity and unlimited potential. This means you have work to do. Please do not misread or misinterpret this.

We all have work to do.

This is not a one-time evaluation either. It should be done repeatedly, at least every six months if you are to create your best decade. Scores in different areas will change depending on what job you are doing, what school you are enrolled in, and which environment you find yourself in. It is an evaluation of your unlimited potential that is always in flux. Your jars are always opening and capping.

Now, why would I title this chapter "Unlimited Potential" if there is a capacity limit for each area of your life and a maximum score on the capacity test? Easy answer.

The day you reach 120 on this evaluation is the day you will realize that you are living to your unlimited potential.

When you get there, only you will know. You will be balanced, efficient, effective, and high functioning in all areas of life. You will conquer each day as if it's your last and you will be surrounded by individuals who are also close to reaching their unlimited potential. As Writer and Author Benjamin Hardy says, you will be in a "peak state" form of living each day. You will feel an internal peace that nothing in the world can take from you. If, and when, you arrive at that destination, you will realize that mastery of capacity equals unlimited potentiality. It is an incredible feeling.

Personally, I have only been at that level a few chapters in my life. It is extremely hard to get to this level of living and even harder to sustain, but it can be done. Keep pushing and pursuing nothing but greatness in these areas, and you will find yourself creating your best decade. It will be an incredible life for you to live!

Now that you have completed an honest evaluation of where your capacity levels lie and how near or far you are from reaching your unlimited potential, it is time to discover the next steps to your best decade. The remaining chapters will be key in helping you close the margin between limited capacity and unlimited potential. That is the margin between being an eighty-five and one hundred and twenty, or *between living a good decade to creating your best decade.*

Enjoy the ride!

CHAPTER 2
Fully Living With Intention

> *"The greatest thing that you can do is to be intentional with everyone around you, including yourself."*

BEFORE READING THIS chapter I would strongly encourage you to read *Intentional Living* by John C. Maxwell. After reading his book at twenty six, it changed my life. Whether you are well before twenty six, or well after, I trust it will change yours too. Now, if you want to set your next decade up for success, increase your influence and capacities in your current decade, or expand beyond the next decade to set yourself up for a smooth 'retirement' phase of life, this chapter will be a tool in your knapsack to help you do so effectively.

I see an increasing problem with society today. We all seem to communicate endlessly, but very few people know the power of their "word". From a young age, my Dad always told me that a man was only as good as his word and I never forgot this. Today, however, I see top companies and apps around the globe that are all trying to tackle communication 'ease' with an approach that suits the needs of each individual. I am here to tell you that although these approaches to communication do help, *they are not the answer to living with intention.* There is a big difference between simply communicating and being intentional with relationships. While technology can give rise to many great things, it does not replace intentionality. Nothing in this world can replace intentionality. Before I tell you how to live intentionally, and why it is tremendously important, let me first define what it means to live with intention.

Intentional living as defined by Google is a bunch of bogus. So, my advice here is to continue reading this chapter before trying to figure this out via Google. To live with intention, you first need to define what your values are, and then you need to define how *you* live by those values. Once you do this you are ready to start **living with intention.** Picture this series of steps as an interconnected triangle. These three elements will allow you to live a life inside the triangle that you truly want. Here is an example:

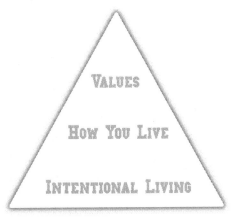

Figure 1: Living With Intention

Every one of us have different values, which can be both core and fluid depending on where we are in life. If you are seventeen, your values may be very different from when you are thirty-nine. Or, you may be thirty one and pregnant, but by thirty two your values have changed while you begin to raise your child. The point here is that values can be in flux as we journey throughout life.

Your best decade contains time when your values, and the values of those you surround yourself with, are in alignment. I will touch on reaching your values in full later. For now, let's stay focused on intentional living. Most people never truly get to a point where they are *actually* living a life of intention. Here's a perfect example: while I was teaching Physical Education in Abu Dhabi, I instructed a swimming unit. Prior to the students' swim test, I had a boy try to convince with me with intense conviction that he was a notable swimmer. Yet I would not allow him in the deep end as he had not passed the basic swim test. I took him aside and explained, *"I know how to cross the street; however, if I know how to cross the street but do not cross properly, is it the same thing?"* My student replied, *"Why would you know how to cross the street, yet not cross properly?"* *"Exactly!"* I replied. *"You tell me that you know and believe that you can swim properly, yet you have not passed the basic swim test. This is why you need to let me teach you how to actually swim properly."* The lesson here was simple: ***Be intentional about what you believe and you can reach the end result.*** Knowing and doing are not the same thing. One without the other is only half of the story. I love teachable moments!

As a matter of fact, most days I am still trying to seek the best ways to live with intention. I have met many people in their sixties and seventies who did not live a life of intention, and it really bothered me to see this at the time. It bothered me because they had so much wisdom, knowledge, and experience to offer the world and those around them, yet never made an intentional effort to make that happen for them in their own lives. What good is knowledge if not shared? If each of us live our lives without intention, we are never going to help ourselves and others achieve their best decade.

For example, do you know someone older than you who does not live with intention? Do they go about their day focused on what *they* need to do instead of strategically and empathetically spending time with loved ones and others around them? If so, go give them a bit of a shake and tell them to wake up. Focus in on investing some quality time with them and show them what it means to live with intention outwardly with others. Serving is a great example of this, and volunteering is a great way to serve others while also being intentional about *how* you are serving others.

Now, most of you probably know someone your age or even younger who does not live with intention on a daily basis. If this is the case, shaking them won't get you anywhere. My best advice for anyone is to make a conscious commitment to yourself, and email me at faheyconsulting@gmail.com to tell me that from this day forward you will make a focused attempt to live with intention. Others around you will start taking notice in three to nine months, and they will start to look at you and say, "Something is different about you, but I don't know what it is." **On that day, you will cross the chasm from just living, to living with intention.** The internal work will become the outward reflection. That is what living with intention looks like.

In 2016 when I was living in Alberta and working as a mentor to schools and teachers I had to get intentional very quickly. I was given a nearly unrealistic task of providing quality mentorship with a wellness lens to teachers and school teams throughout the year in a collective geographic range larger than the countries of Germany, Whales, Malta, Cyprus and the United Arab Emirates combined. I knew this task would test my capacity areas, but I also knew that I had to be incredibly intentional with the job. So, I buckled up and went to work. I took the summer to read and digest "Intentional Living" by John C. Maxwell, changed around my weekly and monthly calendars to become more intentional, cut Facebook and TV out of my life almost completely, and did the following day in and day out for six months:

1. **Defined my values and intentions**
2. **Lived by my values daily, weekly, and monthly**
3. **Repeated the process**

I put a prompt in my work calendar that showed my team I valued spending time thinking about/creating the best results in my life, vocation, and relationships each week. I wanted people close to me to see that I was living with intention. I didn't see the point in leading from the back. For my work, I decided that no matter what I did, I wanted to make a difference by positively affecting change in the way teachers embedded wellness into their teaching. On Sunday evenings, I would close the door to my spare room and spend 30 minutes reviewing these points:

PROFESSIONAL

- Do my tasks this week align with my personal and professional goals?
- If yes, set aside fifteen minutes before each meeting to be 'in the zone' to deliver in that meeting.
- If no, shorten or postpone the meeting to a different time.
- Am I working toward my goals?
- What is time sensitive? How can I get ahead of this early?
- What do I need to book for the next two weeks?
- What have I been putting off that needs attention?

PERSONAL

Am I...

- Becoming a strong leader in physical literacy and wellness
- Becoming family minded
- Becoming a Christ-like man
- Becoming an authentic leader
- Serving my partner
- Who can I reach out to this week to connect with? Why am I choosing to connect with them?
- What have I been putting off that needs attention?

PERSONAL GROWTH

- How can my work this week fuel my growth, hobbies, and passions? Where are there opportunities for growth?
- What can I read/research?
- How can I manage my calendar to create more time for myself?

Yearly theme: Reputation/Legacy

NOTE: *Be Accountable, take responsibility, be intentional*

BIG GOALS FOR THE YEAR

1. **Crush it at work**
2. **Serve my partner**
3. **Focus on the future/generating opportunities**
4. **Work on my Spiritual Life**

After completing this process each week, I noticed a huge difference within six months. It did not happen overnight. Like anything in life, it took time and energy to bring to fruition. After six months, I noticed that I was being taken more seriously; I gained respect within my profession from coworkers as well as those whom I was mentoring at the time. I was on top of due dates, projects, appointments, and meetings, and I also had the highest return of investment (ROI) on my team within that year. Invoices were coming in and phones were ringing daily. People knew I was in the business of adding value to them, and they couldn't get enough of it. It spread as fast as a viral Instagram story.

After making some intentional decisions about how you would like to live by your defined values, the next step is to set a calendar prompt about eight months out from now. This is a great time to check in on your goals of living with intention. Then you can reflect on the areas in which you are succeeding, as well as the areas which may need more attention. Once you establish this list, rank yourself out of 10 and be honest with yourself. Here is an example of my refurbished list and my evaluation technique to establish if I was truly living with intention. Notice that I switched my #1 and #4 in my evaluation and that my list grew as I began to live my life with intention.

1. My Relationship with Christ - 6
2. Serving my future wife - 7.5
3. Crush it at my work - 9.5
4. Connecting with my family & friends - 6.5
5. Setting Amber and I up for success - 9.5
6. Influencing others in a positive way - 9
7. Building my reputation as a leader - 8.5

Also, notice that even though my top two were listed as such, after doing this evaluation I found that I was 'saying' these were my top two values but I wasn't truly being as intentional as I could be. This was a huge gut check for me to step back and realign my values with my evaluation of living with intention. This also showed me that my three lowest rankings were in the emotional area. I had succeeded in crushing it at my work, but other areas were not as strong as they should have been. Then it hit me. *I had to step back professionally to connect more emotionally.* You may find this is true for you as well. Through reflecting, I realized I can easily become so busy and wrapped up with my passions that I forget the importance of connecting emotionally on a daily basis.

Overworked = < Emotional Capacity

This evaluation also revealed to me that I was heading for burnout and needed a change. My future wife and my relationship with Christ were in need of more of my energy, and my intention to connect daily in those areas had declined rapidly. This process helped confirm my decision to move laterally within my field. It was time to step back from my professional commitments.

Try this on your own and see for yourself where and how you may need to realign and shift your energy back to your top three values. I guarantee that it will reveal some things about your intentional values that often get missed in the busyness of life.

The beautiful part of this evaluation for me was that it allowed me to save myself and my future marriage before it was too late. Physiologically I knew I needed a change, but relationally and emotionally I was not seeing it. With this clear evaluation I was able to stop the train before it went off the rails. I am unbelievably grateful for this. I hope it can be a useful evaluation for you as well.

Another important piece of information to note is that your values *will* change. As I mentioned earlier, values change depending on where you are at in your life. Knowing this, I would do this eVALUation about every eight to ten months to see if they have shifted and/or need to be adjusted. Trust me, this will start you off on a positive trajectory in your best decade to keep you grounded when real life hits, and it will keep you stable and sharp later in life.

I do not write this to sound arrogant or to overwhelm you. I am simply reporting this to show you that if a kid from the dirt road could figure this out in his mid-twenties, you can at seventeen, twenty five or fifty five. Always be a student of yourself. Begin by taking everything around you more seriously and you are already on your first step towards living with intention each day. This exercise is meant to be an awakening for you to pause, breathe, and reflect. If you are in your teens, take this and start applying it to your life right now. If you want to be ahead of all of your classmates, I guarantee you that this practice will set you apart from your peers and set you up for a successful and fulfilling life. While your friends are worrying about the latest app for sharing photos, you will be in the trenches putting in the leg work and will eventually have them thinking, "Hey, remember that person who came around a bit, who was really nice and made us feel good when we talked to them? Well apparently they are the CEO of a large organization now." Don't underestimate the importance of starting now. The trajectory to your best decade is found in the breadcrumbs of decisions made now.

To live with intention is a constant practice which ebbs and flows over time. Every day presents new challenges that can drive you away from fully living with intention or not living with intention.

Below is a continuum I created that illustrates the spectrum of intentional living. On the far left we have "NLWI" which stands for "not living with intention." In the middle we have "SLWI" which means "somewhat living with intention" and on the far right we have "FLWI" or "fully living with intention". In the next five minutes, I want you to take personal stock of where you currently fall on this spectrum. Are you consistently living with intention, or do you feel you are falling short in the important areas of your life? Both are ok! Whichever end of the spectrum you find yourself, there is still so much to learn. The best thing about doing this exercise now is that you have the opportunity to recreate the next and most powerful decade of your life by making small, intentional choices now. Tomorrow is a brand new day and you can easily move along the continuum from left to right by tweaking a few things in your day-to-day living.

Figure 2: The Continuum of Living With Intention

If you are not living with intention in a certain area of your life, there is hope and time. With just a few small changes, you can take yourself from not living with intention (NLWI) to somewhat living with intention (SLWI).

If you find yourself in the middle of this spectrum each day, the same is true for you. With the strategies outlined in this book and others, you can make a few tweaks in your day to day living in order to move to the far right in a matter of weeks.

Ultimately, your goal in your best decade is to be as far right as you can be on this continuum each day. I guarantee that if you stay to the far right daily, weekly, and monthly, you will be in for the greatest decade of your life.

If you are in your twenties or thirties and working your first real job outside of formal education, class is not dismissed. You have a tremendous opportunity to lay some serious ground work within your role to become very successful as you move forward in your career and in your relationships.

Or, maybe you are in your forties and you are staring across the kitchen table thinking, "How can I continue to provide for my family if things become tough financially?" Are there intentional steps you need to take to create a better financial situation for yourself and your family?

If you want to be in the industry of creating your best life, living with intention is part of that painful process. Remember, I told you that it took roughly six months to begin seeing the payout of evaluating and adjusting where I put my energy in order to be successful in my twenties. For some of you it may take years; for others, maybe as little as three weeks. Either way, adopting the philosophy of "investing now, reaping later" will provide huge payouts later in life. With all of this, I want to leave you with a powerful thought from this chapter:

Whichever decade you find yourself in, get to work now on creating Your Best Decade (YBD).

CHAPTER 3
The Three Truths of Significance

> *"You need to encourage yourself especially if you know you are on the path of significance."*
> —Sunday Adelaja,
> The Mountain of Ignorance

Now that you have a basic understanding of what it means to live intentionally day in and day out, I want to show you how you can add significance to the big three areas of your life in your best decade. I want you to add significance to yourself, family, friends, colleagues, and profession. Regardless of your title or position, you are capable of adding significance to others every single day.

There are truths in the world that have existed for thousands of years, yet people rarely talk about them. Why? Because some truths are not breaking news. 'Significance' is not a headline story. There is no shock factor attached to this word that draws people in.

But the good news is that I am excited to talk about being a person of significance. Chances are pretty good that this is an important area for you too.

First Truth

Every person on the planet is struggling for significance.

I recently read in Business Insider that Author and Speaker Tony Robbins works sixteen hour days at fifty seven years of age. This man could have retired years ago, yet he continues to work like he's a recent grad trying to establish a name for himself. Why? Because his drive and passion for adding value and significance to others and the world around him pushes him to maximize his days and challenges him to produce amazing work. Iconic! I recently listened to Robert Swan speak at New York University, Abu Dhabi and he left me with a powerful quote: *"Whatever you do, make sure it is relevant. You may think you are doing something relevant, but do you truly know if your work is relevant?"* Be the Tony Robbins to yourself and to those around you. Add value, daily!

We all aim to be significant. Whether that is a significance found within relationships or within our vocations, we aim to be significant within the life we create. Unfortunately, our educational system does not always teach us how to properly add and measure significance in our lives. Without these tools we often fall short, unaware of our true significance to ourselves and to others. If this is you, you are not alone.

If you are one of the lucky ones like me, someone or some people have stumbled into your life from time to time to help you in your quest for significance. This may be the first time you have heard this, but it needs to be said:

You are significant. Give significance to others.
You are significant. Give significance to others.

Powerful words combined for a powerful statement. I want you to repeat this statement daily for the next two weeks. Spread this message on your social media channels. Make these words the slogan for this chapter of your life, also known as your best decade.

We are all significant people, yet we are often focusing on insignificant things. This is why we tend to come up short in having confidence in ourselves and in the work we do. Last year I dealt with a colleague at work who spent numerous hours trying to get what she felt she deserved by consistently taking from others. She would go through her weeks focusing on professionally insignificant things which made her feel significant. The problem was that these personally significant tasks for her, were trivial and insignificant to her colleagues who were trying to get the job done in a supportive environment. The takeaway here is this:

> Be relevant to you, but be significant to others. Feel the rewards of accomplishing significant tasks together, regardless of what you feel is personally relevant.

For example, when you show up for work are you there to "punch the clock" or do you show up ready to add value to others? Do you engage in quality conversation with your colleagues? Are you taking your spouse for granted? Do small things like doing the dishes serve little to no significance in your relationship? Have you stopped carrying out acts of love? Powerful thought! I challenge you to become less complacent and more intentional in adding significance to your relationships, especially with your partner and those closest to you.

You can easily become a person of significance each and every day in all areas of your life, and your profession is no exception. If you don't believe me, let me tell you another story about Mr. Omarz.

While I was working at a School in the Middle East, I had the pleasure of calling Mr. Omarz my colleague. Mr Omarz was one of the most sought after and significant persons in our school. Now, you are probably trying to guess what role Mr. Omarz filled within the school. Being one of the most important figures, was he a Principal? Owner? Curriculum Manager? None of the above, actually. Mr. Omarz was hired to run the photocopy machines for the school. So, on paper Mr. Omarz was likely the "photocopy manager ", if the title was ever formalized. For years Mr. Omarz came and went from his small photocopy room supporting teachers and administrators with all their paper and photocopy needs. He moved fast and was very detail oriented. His ability to efficiently execute tasks was superior. Teachers would come to him in a bind, often needing something photocopied within minutes and Mr. Omarz delivered every day. He never over promised, never complained, never hid behind his desk, and you never had the sense that he was frustrated, overwhelmed, and/or burned out.

Now some of you may be thinking, "Well, that was clearly Mr. Omarz's job. What is the point here? We all work hard regardless of title."

Let me stop you there.

Mr. Omarz did more than just deliver on his job. He added significance to his job day in and day out. What I didn't tell you was that when I would seek Mr. Omarz for assistance, he would greet me with a smile, offer me a treat, and take the time to get to know me, asking about my weekend or about my family. He also went above and beyond his job description when he coordinated trips to Oman for teachers to renew their visas, in order for them to continue teaching in the UAE. Mr. Omarz was much more than a Photocopy Manager. He not only led beyond his title, he was significant to the day-to-day working operations of the school and to all he connected with.

While Mr. Omarz added significance to his job and to others' days, I suspect that many of us are not following this principle. No offense here, but let's be honest with ourselves. Are we carrying ourselves like Mr. Omarz or are we dragging ourselves to and from our jobs mindlessly obeying orders, doing task A, B, and C. Are we able to go above and beyond this level of thinking? Are we adding significance to each customer we greet, each person we meet, and to each task that needs to be done? Our lives are more than just a series of trivial tasks and our days are filled with more than nameless people. We all possess significance and showing that through how you work day in and day out allows you to start building a legacy within your best decade.

One thing I ask myself each day I wake up is, *"How can I add value and significance to others I will meet today?"* When I was teaching, I would be thinking on my walk to work each morning, "How will my students be impacted by me today? How will I add value to their lives and make a significant positive impact on their life?"

I have found that the best way to be significant is for you to be your honest and genuine self each day. Do not try to be someone you are not. People remember fake smiles. People can read through conversations to know if you are trying to sell something or not. People know if you truly care or if you are just asking them questions for information's sake.

Don't be those types of people.

Be significant and add value to others by listening to them, asking them how they feel and how their day is going, or even how they are managing with everything in their lives. Give this a try with someone you see daily and watch what happens next.

Be genuine.

For the most part, people want to be heard, they want to open up, and they want to know they are cared for.

Show empathy.

This takes a bit of time obviously but it is such a rich investment to make if you are going to build a life of legacy that people will remember. Trust me, adding significance and value to others can be a very strong investment.

SECOND TRUTH

People only change because they become motivated through significance.

Let me explain.

A former client of mine lost twenty nine pounds with me as her personal trainer. Despite great loss and emotional lows in her personal life, she still adopted healthy lifestyle choices and stuck with me as her trainer. A few years after our training had finished up, we met up for lunch on the Halifax waterfront. She was calm, poised, radiant, and healthy. She had downsized her house and created a new life for herself in Halifax. Her statements radiated with undertones of wellness, stability, and peace. Beautiful!

I realized something during that lunch. It was the time and significance I invested in her that provided her the motivation that helped her to succeed. I was able to elevate our training sessions from just a physical lens to a wellness lens, adapting our sessions accordingly.

Was I an amazing personal trainer?

Not necessarily.

Was I great at using the intimate personal training platform as a way to constantly add value and significance to her as my client?

Absolutely.

As a matter of fact, I took this approach with another client as well. He was much younger and wondering where his identity laid. He was once a hockey player, but switched to become a badminton player at a pivotal point in his athletic life. While I trained him to build explosive strength and muscular endurance, we also worked on sharpening his mental game. We worked on building his confidence to become the amazing leader and athlete that he was capable of becoming. Two years following our training, we met for coffee where I learned he was competing at the highest level in Collegiate Badminton for his College in Nova Scotia, while simultaneously running competitively on their Cross Country team. Since we last spoke, he recently completed his first marathon in Yarmouth, Nova Scotia. I also received a message from him on Instagram this year which read, "*All your pushes forward brought me to what I am today.*"

Incredible.

I don't write these stories to brag about my clients' successes or my own successes as a trainer. I tell these stories to show you the power of adding significance to others around you. This leads me to my *third truth*:

Significance over time equals optimal results.

Another example of a time I tried to add significance to others was when I travelled to rural communities in northern Alberta for work. A lot of these communities are transient where contractors and workers come in for a few weeks or months, block off some hotel rooms, and then typically leave.

When I started making my trips to Peace River, Alberta, I noticed something strange as I checked into the hotel. The line up for check-in was long and filled with many of these contract workers. One by one they reached the representative at the front desk where they would utter as few words as needed. They would get their keycard and proceed to their room without a simple "thank you" or "see you tomorrow". *It was a simple give and take transaction.*

Noticing this, I made it a point to get to know the front desk representatives and build a bit of a relationship with them in the short time I had. When my turn came, I stepped up to the desk and noticed the representative's name tag. Her name was Delores. I immediately said, "*Good evening Delores, you are a busy woman here tonight.*" She promptly responded with a smile and said, "*Well, yes I am actually. I was called in last minute and I have been run off my feet. Thank you for your patience.*" To which I replied, "*Wow. I am sorry to hear that Delores. It is good to be busy in the hotel industry, but being run off your feet is never fun. I hope you get some rest when your shift is finished.*"

She smiled and handed me my keycard and said, "*Thank you sir, I appreciate that. I will be back in tomorrow so I will see you in the morning. Don't forget to have a good breakfast before you hit the road.*"

Little did I know, I would end up making about fifteen visits to stay at that very hotel the rest of the year. Each time I arrived at the hotel, Delores would immediately ask how I was doing and was genuinely interested in my life. By the end of the year, Delores knew my family, where we lived, what I did for work, and where I was originally from. More importantly though, I felt comfortable seeing a familiar face who always smiled with genuine interest when she saw me. She always went above and beyond her job description. Thank you for teaching us the power of significance, Delores.

Because I took the time to add value to Delores while she was at work, she then put in the extra effort to go above and beyond for me during my work travels. Whereas most people didn't attempt to get to know her, I recognized the importance in her knowing her significance and the role she played during my stay.

The best part of all of this, is that I am not sure if I added value to Delores or if she added value to me. It was a symbiotic transaction of adding significance to each other during our interactions.

Mr. Omarz and Ms. Delores are everywhere in the world. They are the people cleaning your city streets, making sure your water is topped up at your favorite restaurants, and they are the ones making sure your airplane is clean when you get on your flight. Recognize them for the amazing amount of significance they add to the world around them.

In your personal relationships, find ways in which you can live with intention to better add daily significance to them, and better serve their needs lovingly. If you want to create the best decade of your life, doing this is critical. Leadership starts in the home. If you have kids, be more than just a parent. Be a *significant* parent. Use events as teachable moments. Use quality time with your children as a way to build significance in their lives by creating lasting memories. My parents did a wonderful job of this with me, and that is something I am truly grateful for.

In a world that seems to be increasingly pressured by high grades, the latest promotions, awards for performance, and racing to the top as a big CEO, I encourage you to think differently about valuing *significance over reward*. If you add value and make others around you feel significant each day, you are on the path to creating the best decade of your life. It will take years to see this investment mature into a retirable currency but trust me, adding significance to others daily will produce fruitful payoffs for decades to come!

CHAPTER 4
Abundance Thinking

> *"The only thing in the world that is not abundant is the thing you believe not to be abundant. That thing for me is time."*

ONE THING IS for sure. Someday we will all run out of time. It may not be today or tomorrow or ten years from now but, eventually, we will run out. Time is the only currency that is scarce. Everything else in life is abundant. Now that we have established this, let's unpack how you can live your best decade through an abundance mindset.

You know the feeling. You reach for that jar of peanut butter only to find it almost empty. Or you finally sit down to your favorite meal at your favorite restaurant when you reach for the red ketchup bottle only to find that even though it is red, there is hardly any ketchup inside the container. Awful trickery! **Scarcity results are let downs in life.** Who wants to see a small puddle of water in the desert? Wouldn't you rather come across a gigantic lake of fresh water instead? Oddly enough, we tend to see the puddles more than the lakes within our lives. Will I have enough gas for the trip? Will I be able to make ends meet? Will I have work in my future? These are all questionable manifestations of our scarcity thinking.

Scarcity thinking is so easy.

It is abundance thinking that is actually more challenging to bring into your life.

I want to talk to you about what happens when scarcity thinking is minimal. Let's talk about the feeling you get when you know the jar is full and when you know that the work will be there, and how this can impact your well-being in the best decade of your life. Before we journey there, however, I need to share some insight with you about scarcity mindset. Scarcity exists. There was a time in human history where people feared venturing out too far out of fear of a flat world that would be barren and scarce in supplies. That all changed when one man and his crew courageously sailed beyond this fear and proved the world was indeed round.

Humanity shifted from scarcity to abundance.

Are you in the boat exploring new boundaries or are you on the shore fearful that those in the boat will never be seen again?

Finances

Scarcity is a lacking or short supply of something in our lives. (Source: http://www.dictionary.com/browse/scarcity). Most commonly, I see this mindset swell up in two main areas of a person's life.

First, I see it in the way people discuss their finances and plan their spending habits. The majority of arguments that couples have in their relationship are due to finances. The largest factor in our decision-making process comes from a financial angle. That is also wise. What is not wise is thinking that there is, "*just barely enough*" or thinking, "*I am not sure if we can make it.*"

In the best decade of your life, you will have abundance. How do I know this? Because if you put into practice the tools I give you throughout this book, you will find yourself in a much better position in many areas of your life within a few weeks or months. I love the story in the Bible when Jesus turned just a few fish and loaves of bread into enough food to feed thousands of people. During scarce times, he showed us the ultimate form of abundance mindset in combination with generating miracles.

CAREER DECISIONS

Second, I see a scarcity mindset in how people make career and job decisions. I will touch on this in more detail later when I talk with you about the stories we tell ourselves, but for now let's just take a moment to unpack this area as it pertains to abundance thinking.

First, let's talk about how many times you have said the following statements either internally or externally resulting from a *scarcity* mindset:

"*No, I can't apply for this job. It doesn't have the security I have now and if I leave I can never come back.*" - Scarcity Thinking

"*There may not be enough people signed up ahead of time for my class so I may have to cancel.*" - Scarcity Thinking

"I am not going to apply for that promotion because I doubt I will get it. There are many more qualified people than me." - Scarcity Thinking

These two are my personal favorites:

"I wanted to buy that new book but instead I decided to wait until I have more money." - Scarcity Thinking

"I want to write a book but who would buy it?" - Scarcity Thinking

---

Now, let's look at these statements from an *abundance* mindset:

"There seem to be endless opportunities out there for me. I should apply with the intention of moving to this position and if it doesn't work out I will still gain experience from this." - Abundance Thinking

"My class will reach at least minimum capacity each week so I need to be prepared to run a great set of classes that are engaging and scalable." - Abundance Thinking

"Who better to receive a promotion than me? I am fully confident that I will receive a promotion. It is just a matter of time." - Abundance Thinking

"Buying books is an investment in my future and my future is bright. I will buy at least one now that will set me up for more amazing books to come." - Abundance Thinking

"I have a story to tell and maybe I am the next Dr. Seuss."
- Abundance Thinking

Do you see the difference?

The glass is only half empty if you choose to see it as half empty.

It is totally up to you and your perception.

Will it be abundant or scarce?

I remember running the Spartan Beast event with my brother-in-law in August of 2017 in Quebec, Canada. The course was a nightmare and as prepared as I was, I still knew it would be a real grind and expose my weaker areas. I had plenty of supplies with me for the projected four to five hour race. With each ascent and obstacle that we completed, I felt good about where we both were mentally and physically within the race. I was excelling in the obstacles and I was confident we would finish the course within our projected time goal.

Photo: Bucket Brigade obstacle
during the 5th hour of the QC Spartan Beast

However, we soon found ourselves approaching the last and most grueling part of the race at five hours and fifteen minutes. Our supplies were getting low and our GPS systems were a bit miscalculated due to the canopy of trees and rocks we were weaving around. About 18 km into the 23 km race, my mind started to switch from abundance thinking to scarcity thinking. I was running low on water, electrolyte supplies, and energy gels that had been fueling us from kilometer one. My brother-in-law was also getting low, but I knew he was in much better shape with his supplies. The longer we remained on that ridge, the longer I needed to ration my supplies to ensure that I had more than enough for the final push. I immediately recognized this thinking and started talking to myself out loud. I kept repeating, "*It can't be that much longer. I only need just enough supplies to make it. I can make it. I will endure this. I am good. I am good.*" At one point my brother-in-law slowed down and patted me on the back and asked, "*You good?*"

My response was, "*I am still effective brother.*"

I think we both recognized our current situation and our dwindling supplies, but we both knew we would finish the race, even if one of us needed to carry the other over the finish line.

Photo: Monkey Bar climb
at 950m elevation during Spartan Beast race in Quebec

Sure enough, we started our final descent and had about 1.5 km to go when I took my last energy chew. We split what was left of a LARABAR, and crossed the finish line with nothing left between us but about a quarter of that last bar. Now, that's what I call scarcity! Had we run out, my legs would have seized up on the mountain and it would have been a bad sight. Had he run out, who knows for how long he would have the carbohydrates and sugars he needed to finish the race. The critical moment when scarcity mindset takes over is scary and it can become infectious. It starts with one situational context and then moves into another. Being mindful of this is key. You don't have to believe everything that your mind tells you. Let me say that again: *you don't have to believe everything your mind tells you.* That day the glass was half full until I ran low on the supplies my body demanded of me. But I still had to remind myself that I would be ok and that I had *enough* to make it to the finish! I had to practice an abundance mindset with every step for the last hours of the course.

Photo: My brother-in-law (David Enman) and I crossing the finish line after 6+ hours of Spartan racing.

I recall another time earlier in my career when an abundance mindset was very important. I was driving from Washington, D.C, to Raleigh, North Carolina, and my director and I were stuck on the I-95, which was backed up in Quantico due to mass construction. We were talking the whole way back about work, life, and what we were going to do in N.C when we suddenly realized that we were running low on gas. My director was driving and I was in the passenger seat having a mild panic attack. We had only 10 km left in the tank and traffic was at a stand still. I spent the next 10 km in distress as we literally crawled on what little fuel remained. I was already developing a plan of attack for what we would do when we ran out of gas. I remember looking over at my director when the meter read 2 km until empty. He was not bothered by it at all and said, "*We will find something Ryan, don't worry.*" Meanwhile, I was frantic.

Sure enough, we pulled into a gas station on the right-hand side of the freeway as the gas meter read 0 km until empty. He put the van in park at the pump, looked at me, smiled, and said, "*See Ryan, I told you we would be ok.*" He did not let scarcity mindset and anxiety take over his thinking and his conversations. He was "as cool as a cucumber" during that whole situation. He always displayed an abundance mindset which was really admirable, especially as an example to see early in my career. The glass was always half full for him, and I appreciated learning under his authentic leadership.

Photo: Me (left), Artie Kamiya (Center), Father of Physical Education in America, Rich Rairigh (Right), Director of Be Active Kids in Raleigh, NC.

Recently, I have seen amazing results in taking an abundance mindset approach in every area of my life. This hasn't been easy. There are times I still question myself and my ability to achieve a specific goal; however, I try to be mindful in those moments to set myself up to think with a greater abundance mindset. For example, I recently felt a huge amount of tension and stress in my life with regards to my career. Having only worked a brief two years at this organization, I wondered if I should ask for a leave of absence. Financially, I had to get paid as I still had massive student loan debt (*which I am sure all of you post secondary millennials know all about*). I started exploring job opportunities that would allow me to take a leave to focus on my health, my values, and my book. I talked things over with my partner. We came to the conclusion that we wanted to travel, save money, and experience different cultures in a warmer climate, all before starting a family. In our current situation, we were not able to do that as effectively as we had hoped. So, I threw my name abroad and connected with friends and former colleagues in warmer climates that were central to good travel destinations. From here, we opened the gates to our available options.

Realizing the world was open to us, we made inroads with some of our connections. Within a matter of weeks, we both found jobs in our chosen professions. I would teach and my partner would work with me internationally in Abu Dhabi. Knowing this, I proposed a leave of absence to my boss which would allow me to take a year to teach abroad, and he went for it. Because I used an abundance mindset in my decision making, I set us up to continue to reach our goals on the international stage.

In proposing the leave, I trusted that what I brought to the table would be enough for my employers to see the value in a leave. I wanted breathing room and space to explore the world, grow internationally, and bring even more skills and knowledge to the table upon my return to Canada.

I could have said, "*Well honey, what we have now is really good. Maybe we can travel in two more years.*" Or I could have said, "*Honey, I am too scared to ask for a leave because I haven't been there that long. I don't know if my boss will go for it.*" Instead, I threw the Hail Mary and made the winning throw. I sought the win/win I was looking for, for both my organization and for our lives, and executed on our move to Abu Dhabi. **That day my world changed because I** *switched from scarcity thinking to abundance thinking in my professional life.*

All of this was due to using an abundance mindset (*and a dose of courage*). I trusted that we would land on our feet. I also had a little help from two great authors. I wanted to prepare a solid case for our decision to move laterally by reading *The Dip* By Seth Godin and *The 4-Hour Workweek* by Timothy Ferriss. These two books changed my thinking and expanded my professional capacity to see the world and the opportunities the world provides with a different mindset.

Abundance thinking works. It changes the course of your life and can improve your quality of life day in and day out in your best decade. In your own life, you may be looking at post-secondary options.

What schools can I go to after high school?

Am I good enough for XYZ University?

Will I land the job I want?

Will I get the next promotion in my office?

Let me throw some interesting stats to you. As of 2017, there are over twenty three thousand Universities in the world (Source: http://www.webometrics.info/en/node/54). If University isn't for you and you are looking to go to a college or institute: as of 2016 there were one hundred and ten registered colleges in Canada alone (Source: http://www.studyincanada.com.ng/universities-and-colleges/colleges-in-canada.html). There are tons of places for you to study and pursue the education you'd like. Simply put, there is an abundance of levels of education, types of education, and institutions that are looking for you.

Maybe you are in your late twenties or early thirties and still single. Maybe you are wondering if you will ever find that Mr. or Mrs. Right. You may be thinking that you have tried everything and that you don't think the right person is out there for you. Maybe you are having doubts that the options are scarce because all of your friends are married and some even have kids. This can be frustrating and challenging for sure. However, what if you replace your scarcity thinking with an abundance mindset? You could then be thinking, "*There are tons of options in the world for me. I just can't wait to find my perfect option. It will happen when it is meant to happen.*" The world is a big place and as of late 2017, there are about 7.8 billion people on the planet. Whatever or whomever you want to pursue, the options are all there for you. Be patient and be thinking with abundance!

Maybe you are in your late thirties or early forties and wondering if you missed the boat on having kids. I would encourage you to tackle that thinking and pursue the goals that you and your partner have for a family. There are plenty of adoption agencies to choose from. It is not too late for you and your family! Make decisions from an abundance mindset and enjoy the payoffs that life can offer you.

Whatever challenges lie ahead or whatever obstacle arises in your life, taking this mindset with you through those situations and chapters of your life will help you live an abundant life filled with well-being in your best decade.

> If X doesn't work out for one reason or another, remember that option Y just might work out down the road for you.

Every closed door may lead to an open window in your best decade.

Things may not always work out as you imagined, but if you choose to take the perspective of an abundance mindset, everything works out as it should. There are always options when you adopt this mindset.

Having a high spiritual sense can help as well. For example, one of my mentors once told me, "*Ryan, Rejection is God's Highest Form of Protection.*" Now, you may share different beliefs but the point here is that if you embrace your spirituality, evaluate your beliefs, and move forward in your life with the next option from an abundance mindset, it will serve you in your best decade. Some doors will open, others may close, but if you have an *unshakeable abundance thinking mindset* the opportunities behind a multitude of doors are essentially endless as you continue to create your best decade. To keep it simple:

Abundance thinking over time produces great results.

Great results lead to more great opportunities.
More great opportunities creates a richer life in your best decade.

A richer, more fulfilling life keeps you on the path to living your best decade.

My challenge to you is quite simple. The next time you find yourself thinking with a scarcity mindset, or you see yourself acting out of scarcity rather than abundance, check your thinking and reset your thoughts to abundance before you make a decision. This will be a key piece for you to master if you are to sustain the ups and downs that will arise in your best decade.

CHAPTER 5
Legacy > Resume

> *"My mother always told me that as you go through life, no matter what you do, or how you do it, you leave a little footprint, and that's your legacy."*
>
> —Jan Brewer

Is YOUR LEGACY greater than your resume?

Are you willing to invest in people rather than how you look on paper?

Are you interested in serving yourself or serving others?

If you can answer these questions honestly, you are ready to create a legacy that is much greater than your resume.

Legacy is defined as something handed down or received from an ancestor or predecessor. (Source: https://www.dictionary.com/browse/legacy). Simply put, what you leave behind when you move on from an Organization, Institution, Community, or place of influence *defines* your legacy. This is vital for you to learn in your teens, practice in your twenties, and intentionally pass along in your thirties, forties, and beyond.

Before we get too deep into legacy, let me share a story with you that I once read in the *4-Hour Workweek* by Timothy Ferriss.

An American Investment Banker was at the pier of a small coastal Mexican village when a small boat with just one fisherman docked. Inside the small boat were several large yellowfin tuna. The American complimented the Mexican on the quality of his fish and asked how long it took to catch them.

The Mexican replied, "Only a little while." The American then asked why he didn't stay out longer and catch more fish? The Mexican said he had enough to support his family's immediate needs. The American then asked, "But what do you do with the rest of your time?"

The Mexican fisherman said, "I sleep late, fish a little, play with my children, take siestas with my wife, Maria, stroll into the village each evening where I sip wine, and play guitar with my amigos. I have a full and busy life."

The American scoffed, "I am a Harvard MBA and could help you. You should spend more time fishing and with the proceeds, buy a bigger boat. With the proceeds from the bigger boat, you could buy several boats, eventually, you would have a fleet of fishing boats. Instead of selling your catch to a middleman you would sell directly to the processor, eventually opening your own cannery. You would control the product, processing, and distribution. You would need to leave this small coastal fishing village and move to Mexico City, then LA, and eventually New York City, where you will run your expanding enterprise."

The Mexican fisherman asked, "But, how long will this all take?"

To which the American replied, "15 – 20 years."

"But what then?" Asked the Mexican.

The American laughed and said, "That's the best part. When the time is right you would announce an IPO and sell your company stock to the public and become very rich, you would make millions!"

"Millions – then what?"

The American said, "Then you would retire. Move to a small coastal fishing village where you would sleep late, fish a little, play with your kids, take siestas with your wife, stroll to the village in the evenings where you could sip wine and play your guitar with your amigos."

Our world today is fast moving and it causes us to constantly adapt. We move from school to school, community to community, and job to job, sometimes overnight. It is not uncommon in 2019 to see someone go from working for Apple in Silicon Valley to running their own Startup in Columbia weeks later. We can create amazing lives and opportunities much faster than we were able to generations ago. However, all of this opportunity comes at a price. That cost can be *legacy*.

I am going to be brutally honest and say that I think a lot of people come and go from school, places of work, and even relationships without establishing a great legacy. Sometimes there is no positive legacy left at all. For instance,

I have seen many teens take on seasonal jobs, work only the hours they are paid for, spend their breaks on their iPhone SM channels and then leave at the end of the summer having accomplished nothing more than a transaction of time for money.

Have they left a legacy? Absolutely not.

Anyone in the world could come in and do the same level of transactional work.

I have seen many people in their twenties begin jobs and have unrealistic expectations. Yes, I am a millennial and we millennials tend to expect the ways to be set, the doors to be open, and the promotions to dance in front of us after six months. When this doesn't happen, we become rigid and entitled to what *we* want and often walk away from a position and leave the infrastructure of that position in professional shambles. This leaves the next person who comes in responsible for not only learning the new job, but also cleaning up our mess.

You may have a fantastic resume, but our world is a global world, so your legacy is not something you can run from. Do yourself a favor and don't create a legacy that you NEED to run from. Create a legacy that constantly runs back to you.

Legacy

I have also come across many people in their twenties, thirties and forties who are trying so hard to climb the professional ladder and build their resume that they forget about their families along the way. Their relationship with their significant other fades, and they end up abandoning their relational duties as they pursue their professional dreams and aspirations. But I have to ask these folks, what legacy are you really leaving?

What about your partner's heart and emotional well-being? Will the next person who enters their lives be forced to attempt to repair a heart that was put in disarray due to mismatched values? What kind of legacy is this?

These above examples are just a few that I have seen. These may not all apply to you, but I hope you get the message loud and clear on what it means to leave an incredible legacy or no legacy at all.

I once knew someone who had a stacked resume. For his own protection, I won't mention his name, but to make a long story short, he had an impressive background in growing successful business ventures on the international stage. He took over a leadership role at a University and ran himself into the ground in a couple of years. No student spoke highly of him, and people felt uncomfortable around him. Although on paper this man had achieved great things, he soon found himself trapped in an envelope of bad legacy where people would rather avoid him than work with him.

One day we woke up and he was gone. No one really noticed that he was gone either. Maybe it was a situation where he was just the wrong person for the job, but the point here is that his legacy quickly caught up to him and sealed him hard in his tracks. He needed to run away from his own legacy and couldn't seem to run fast enough. Don't be that person.

Inversely, there are leaders that shape you, challenge you, and transform you with their sheer presence. My former mentor, employer, and track coach was one of those people. I could spend days writing about all the lessons he taught me and about all the ways he shaped me. However, for the sake of time, I will share only a couple of ways he left a positive and lasting legacy with me and with many in our small, Nova Scotia community.

My mentor's name was Grant MacDonald. He was an unassuming, coffee drinking, six foot five man who brought a calm, collected, and powerful presence to anywhere he went. One of the areas he left a legacy with me was how he handled his work. I remember one time he brought me along to show me what his job was all about. We were outside in a backfield one fall afternoon, and he asked me if I could go to the car to grab a tripod to add to his waypoint. Yes, you guessed it - he was a land surveyor. I immediately took off running towards the car to get the tripod. I got about four or five strides in when I heard him yell at me, *"Ryan - don't ever run on the job if you are getting paid by the hour."* I never forgot that. There have been times in the last decade of my life's work where I inevitably had to run to and from somewhere on the job to complete time sensitive tasks; however, every single time I find myself doing this I am reminded of his brash advice that day after school in the eighth grade.

He taught me that quality work was much richer in value than high quantities of work done poorly. To this day, I still believe in quality over quantity.

On another occasion, he contracted me out to do a land survey job at one of the beaches on the Northumberland Strait in Nova Scotia. I showed up on time with my backpack in hand and raincoat on. I entered his house and asked his wife where he was and if he was ready for work. She said, *"I think he's down in his office in the basement. Take your boots off and go see him if you'd like."* So, I took my boots off, patted their dog a couple of times, and went downstairs only to find him with his feet up watching an indoor track and field race he had taped. He said, *"Come on into my office Ryan. Pull up a seat; we have lots of work to do."* So, I pulled up an old wooden chair and sat beside him. We proceeded to watch this track race and analyzed the times, passes made, splits for each lap of the long distance races in the meet and, before we knew it, it was time for lunch. He looked over at me and said, *"Well Ryan, it looks like it's still raining outside, maybe we can grab some lunch and then head out in the afternoon to do this beach survey."* So, we gathered our equipment, got in the car, and drove down to his favorite restaurant for lunch.

After lunch, we took the back roads to the work site, taking time to indulge in nature's beauty along the way. We stopped to watch an eagle sore and a bear on the side of the road. Finally, at about two o'clock, we made it to the beach, pulled the map out, and drove around until we found our specific work site. We hooked up the instrument, took a couple of infrared shots of three corners of a cottage, packed up the gear, and headed for the cottage we were surveying. We were greeted at the door by a very nice elderly lady who offered us some homemade cookies and tea. He looked at me and then looked at his watch and said, *"I think we have time for cookies and tea, yes."*

So, in we went. We sat, we talked, and we ate her scrumptious cookies. When 3:30 pm rolled around he said, "*Well, it looks like we need to get going.*" We left her cottage, got in the car, and drove back to his home office by 4:30 pm. He looked at me and said, "*Well Ryan, good work today. Same time again next week?*"

I couldn't believe it. I worked thirty minutes over an entire day, ate lunch for free, and got to watch some track and field along the way!

I was blown away!

What I didn't realize was that he was teaching me another lesson. He taught me that some days will not go as planned and you just have to roll with the cards you are dealt by playing them in your favour. This is a critical lesson to learn in your best decade. Sometimes you will not be happy with the cards in your hand, but you still must play the game of life.

In all of these instances, he was teaching me and leaving behind a legacy. I was very young and green, as you may say, to the idea of working for a living. He knew by the way I competed in sport and by my study habits that I was an extremely driven person. He was trying to show me to slow down, smell the roses, and embrace the small joys that life has to offer. All of his numerous lessons have stuck with me to today.

Both on and off the track, he was a transformational leader who left a great legacy with me that I hope to someday pass on to others through this book.

In our community, people still speak of him today even though he has been gone for over eight years. His style of coaching, infectious philosophy around training and race preparation, true resilience to be himself, along with his ability to bring the best out in others was incredible.

> You know you have done something right when people still speak of you in a positive manner around their dinner table ten years after you are gone.

After coaching me in track and field, he went on to coach numerous other middle and long distance runners in the community. One of his athletes even set a provincial record for the 800m distance, which went unbeaten for four years. It wasn't until I met some of his old friends that I came to learn that he himself was a distance running record holder in Nova Scotia for quite some time. For training, he used to run down the streets of our hometown in snow that was sometimes so deep that he would have to match his stride and follow his tracks on his way back just to save energy by not losing his footing in the deep snow. The more I thought about it, the more I realized this lesson.

If your influence can outlive you, you have the ability to leave an incredible legacy.

We often think of great presidents, like President Barack Obama, and famous leaders, such as authors and movie stars, to be the ones who leave a legacy through their work and life. They use their platform to leave a legacy for others. *Everyone is capable of leaving a great legacy, but some leave their legacy in a spotlight.*

Will Smith is a great example of this. Some of the stories and concepts that he shares on his Instagram page are simple and easy to apply to your life. In fact, if he was reading this book he would likely agree with most of my messages for you. However, Will has a much larger spotlight than a first-time author. He can create massive shifts in a lot of people's thinking because he can reach so many, so easily. Keep up the great work, Will!

You also have a great legacy to pass on to others as you begin to build your life, brighten your spotlight, shape your career, and invest in your relationships in your best decade. As you gain greater influence with your family, your circle of friends, colleagues, and employers, your level of influence becomes greater.

This is why teaching is still one of the noblest professions in the world. Every single day you have a multitude of opportunities to leave a great legacy for your students to take, apply, and give back to someone else in their own lives. I know many teachers who have left a great legacy of leadership for me to pick up and add to my knapsack in my best decade.

Yours can be similar!

Nurses also tend to be in great positions to leave a legacy each day. Why do you think I picked a nurse as a life partner? They see so many patients and have very intimate interactions with them when they are arguably at their most vulnerable. Nurses are compassion drivers who have the ability to change a patient's life through a series of empathic interactions.

I remember my partner calling me after her last nursing shift in Lloydminster, Saskatchewan. She was almost speechless. I could not figure out why she didn't seem excited about her final shift, when indeed she was actually overwhelmingly speechless. After working at the Lloydminster Hospital for only about two years, she had been presented with numerous treats, gifts, and send off messages from fellow colleagues, physicians, and from her patients. She had not expected this. I reassured her of her unique skill set and of the value that she added to the hospital, its staff, and their patients.

> Sometimes we forget about how much value and significance we add to others around us, especially in our place of work.

There was a period in my life when I was unwell and had to spend months in a hospital. I still remember the faces of the nurses who were empathetically patient with me, the nurses who were diligent in their practice, and the nurses who helped and guided me when I needed it most.

Some nurses who had been practicing for only three to four years, had left a greater legacy with me than other nurses who had been in the profession for over ten years. ***Legacy is always greater than resume.*** Please remember this as you approach this next decade with vigor, compassion, and love.

Another way to leave a great legacy through your work is to adopt this philosophy early on in your career:

> Finish better than you start.

This was an expression that I needed to put into practice many times in my career. Instead of simply showing up and doing a job, I would commit to having a powerful influence on the direction of the work, by adding authenticity to the positions I earned. For example, when I was working as a Trainer in North Carolina, I tried hard to build genuine, deep relationships with clients so that when I saw them at different conferences across the state, they felt a sense of comfort in knowing a genuine and familiar face. I wanted them to know that I also cherished them outside of work hours. I always made a strong effort to go above and beyond the typical trainer-client relationship with each of them wherever and whenever I could.

While in Alberta, following the approval of my leave to teach internationally, I made an intentional effort to bring all of our new team hires up to speed as fast as I could before I left. I could have simply sat back and coasted into my leave. I could have punched the clock each day and just fulfilled the status quo knowing that I was transitioning into a new professional role for a while. However, I decided not to entertain this mindset. It didn't feel right for me to coast in and out of a job. So, I did the complete opposite. I spent that summer working with my team by diving into resource development, organizing critical planning meetings, and holding weekly one-on-one meetings to make sure they were comfortable making the transition into the upcoming school year. I also invested in them, as people, by connecting them with local places to explore, fitness communities to join, and networks of relationships to tap into in order for them to feel comfortable while also becoming successful. I wanted to leave a legacy of being the best leader I could be to my team while I was able to work alongside them during this transition phase. The last thing I wanted was for the team to be circling the room six months after I left, wondering where things were left and how to reach out to contacts in the communities I had worked closely with. I wanted the opposite for them. I wanted them to be able to start strong and to build the relationships they needed to succeed, and for the organization to move forward. Which leads me to this idea for your best decade:

For all of you teens and young adults reading this, bring this thinking to your schools first. Schools can be great agents of change. You can bring a lot to your school leaders and help take them to the next level. Launch student leaders into their best decade. Find a committee to join, run for your students' council, join various sports teams, or start a club. Find ways to leave a legacy before you walk across the stage at your convocation.

To all of you twenty or thirty somethings, I can't stress this enough. You are at a point in your lives where you have a tremendous opportunity to build a lifelong legacy of leadership that will start running towards you, as opposed to needing to run away from it. The value and significance you bring to your vocation will always carry you further than the bullet points on your resume.

Which leads me to my next thought:

You should be running towards your best decade, not from it.

If you are early into your best decade and happen to be in a position of leadership within your work, try seeking out others in your circle who are leaving positive legacies wherever they drop their suitcases. They will take you and your goals much further in a world in need of increasing transparency and relationship-based, transformational services.

If you are later in your best decade, give the skills and stories you have learned along the way to those just beginning their journey. Empower them to focus on building a life that has a legacy rather than simply helping them with their resume. You have a tremendous gift of experience and time to give to others. Make great use of this time and transfer those stories to others.

Now, how would you market yourself as a person who leaves a greater legacy than their resume? That is probably a question most of you are looking to answer. The answer is multifaceted and not a one-size-fits-all, 'check the box' answer. If you are to create your best decade, here are my top four ideas on how to market yourself as an individual who leaves a greater legacy than resume.

First – Get to Employers

Find a way to call them and email them until they have no choice but to respond to you, and pester them almost to the point of becoming annoying. Get to the annoying line and flirt with it. If you are able to secure facetime with a prospective employer or big influencer in your area of passion, they will find that you are much more than a few bullets highlighted on your resume. Any time I have met with a person of influence, I never brought a resume with me. I, typically, just sat back and had a relaxing conversation with them about their passions, their experiences, and their values. I spent a lot of those face-to-face meetings asking them more questions than they would ask me. I wanted to show them that I cared and that I would bring value to them as a person, and to any position they had vacant.

Second – Thank People

Thank people for meeting with you and for taking time out of their day. Acknowledge that they lead busy lives and that this meeting meant a lot to you. You can thank them at the beginning of the conversation or at the end. Either way, let them know you care and respect their level of influence and their time. Always follow up a meeting or a conversation with a genuine thank you.

Third – Be Early

One of my favorite NHL coaches is Stanley Cup Champion Coach Mike Babcock (*See his book in my book recommendations section*). He always told his players that if they were five minutes early for practice, they were on time. Be early, show them you value them by beating them to the meeting space. What a great way to leave a wonderful first impression. Being in your best decade does not equal being late for a meeting.

Fourth – Character References

Leave detailed references who can speak to your character and to your work. I used to get all hung up on character references versus 'professional' references like they teach us in school. Now I think those titles are actually irrelevant. If you are leaving a legacy, anyone should be able to speak to you as a person and to what you are capable of doing. Character references should not exist as a title in your best decade. Anyone should be able to speak to you positively. Just choose the best spokesperson wisely.

Now, if you are on the opposite side of the spectrum here, how would you look for someone who leaves a greater legacy than a resume? You actually have it easier than those looking to share their legacy with you.

Why?

Because they have left a decorated trail, you just need to find it. I don't think employers spend enough time on this part of the hiring process, and so they often end up settling for mediocre employees who 'just get the job done'. If I were looking for someone of good integrity with a good legacy, I would first search as far back as high school.

Were they a leader then?

What did they do differently back then to separate themselves from their peers?

Do they have humble beginnings?

I would also search each of their previous employment opportunities to make sure they all exist, and to see if there are any testimonials left of them about their work ethic, drive, performance, etc.

Additionally, I would interview the candidate multiple times. When I was going through the application process for my first 'real job' outside of University, my eventual employer conducted three, one-hour Skype interviews with me. I was sure I had the job until I got an email from him saying that he wanted a fourth interview. I was floored, nervous, and apprehensive, but I proceeded with the fourth interview which included their funder. It was as smooth as the first three and I finally landed the job, which I was technically not qualified for. They wanted someone with a Masters Degree, and I was fresh out of my Education Bachelor level degree.

Six months into my position, I asked my director why he needed the fourth interview and he said, *"I knew you were the whole package regardless of your true qualifications, but our funders had to see that as well."*

Legacy is greater than resume. I was underqualified on paper, yet still made the cut. You can too!

Lastly, I would call their references (*of course*) and try to have a genuine conversation with them. We are a product of our environment (*both good and bad*), and if you get a good sense from their references that they will add value to your organization, you probably have yourself a winner. If you feel something isn't right in your gut, you may want to rethink your decision. As David Mamet once referenced in *Tribe of Mentors* by Timothy Ferriss,

"If there is a doubt; there is no doubt."

Wherever you are currently in your life and in your career, do not get discouraged. Be comfortable stepping out and be comfortable knowing that as long as you choose to do the right things, with the right mindset, and the right amount of drive, you can accomplish virtually anything. Great employers want integrity and legacy around them more than they need a worker to 'just do the job'. They may not always say it, but deep down that is truly what everyone wants in a world stuck in the surface level satisfaction of mediocrity. Bring everything you can to your current job today and start seeing what happens. Add value to those you interact with, work alongside, and influence. If you are cutting grass as a summer job, find ways to bring value to that work and leave a legacy. If you are a high-end business owner making million dollar transactions, take some time each week to get to know your staff on a more personal level. Don't simply throw money at them and tell them that they are doing a good job. Get to know them. Make them feel valued. That will allow your business to continue to grow and add to your legacy as a business owner.

If you are reading this and you have family at home, remember that each day you can add value and build a legacy for them. I know people who wake up at 4:30 am during the cold Canadian winter months to run five kilometers in the dark before driving their children to 6:00 am hockey practice. All of this happens before they even start their forty hour work week. They have this schedule about six months a year. Leave a legacy for your family to step into with you.

I want to leave you with this reflection work to help guide you to live a life that adds to a great legacy in your best decade through to the end of your life. Answer these following questions truthfully about yourself either in this book or on your sketchpad:

1. Are you working just to work, or are you intentionally trying to bring value and leadership to your position? If so, use the space below or your own sketchpad to highlight some of the ways you are bringing value to your position each day.

2. Do you feel as though you are creating a lasting legacy that is beneficial to future employment? Good for your relationships? If not, what are some things you could take from this chapter to help improve on your ability to create a lasting legacy?

CHAPTER 6
Take Your Temperature

ONGRATULATIONS, YOU HAVE officially reached the halfway point of this book. You have already unlocked five chapters of advice to apply to your best decade. Just for this, I want you to take a photo of you reading this book and email it to me at faheyconsulting@gmail.com. You can also post a photo of you with this book by using **#YourBestDecade** on any social media platform. I promise to respond to each picture that is sent to me and to post it on my website and twitter page as well. Go ahead, get creative!

Before we go on with the learning, let's take your temperature. Take a moment to think about some of the key pieces that you learned in the first half of this book. What was revealed to you?

In the next half of this book, you will learn how to shift your mindset, burn boats, build bridges, and find ways to become the hungriest person you know. Get ready to bring some oxygen to the flame which will burn brighter in your best decade.

It is time for you to move into the second half of this book. It is even more powerful than the first half. Why?

Because now I am going to give you some serious concepts, stories, and challenges that will push you outside of your comfort zone in your best decade. By the time you do the work in the second half of this book, you will be a different person. You spent the first half of this book working on your mindset and thinking about the world from a different lens through adding value in the 'big three' areas of your life. Now it is time to dig deeper for the results you want within your best decade.

Let's go!

CHAPTER 7
Burn Boats Not Bridges

> *"The hero and the coward both feel the same thing, but the hero uses his fear, projects it onto his opponent, while the coward runs. It's the same thing, fear, but it's what you do with it that matters."*
>
> —Cus D'Amato

THERE IS A provoking story about Hernando Cortez who was sent from Spain to conquer new lands. Upon landing on the beaches of Vera Cruz, Mexico, he had little resources and was vastly outnumbered. He wanted to use fear as a motivator to conquer the new land, so he ordered his men to burn their boats. His enemies, who had previously held the advantage in numbers, saw this and began to fear for their lives. (Source: https://www.robinsharma.com/article/burn-your-boats).

Cortez told his men that there was no going back; no other option but to move forward and conquer the land for Spain. Boats aflame, they charged towards their enemy with a vigor and ferociousness the enemy had never seen before. Cortez and his men overtook the enemy that day and successfully made landfall with their limited resources and small number of men. The ultimate lesson here, is that sometimes in life you are faced with seemingly unbeatable challenges that create defining moments, changing the trajectory of your life. We may be scared to advance, or have fear of the unknown when abandoning our comfort zone, but it must be done.

Be ready for these moments in your best decade.

Boats

There are likely some boats in your life that you need to burn, and there will also be moments in life that you must simply burn the boats. There is a distinct difference between both of these situations.

My job here is to show you that difference and to help guide your future decision making processes to make sure that you burn a boat, not a bridge. First, let's talk about some boats that may need burning.

Relationships

I am going to be bold here. If you are in a toxic relationship, it may be time to burn that boat. If you are working a dead-end job, it may be time to burn that boat as well, before the boat sinks. Don't believe me? Read *The Dip* by Seth Godin.

HOBBIES

If you are wasting time on a hobby that you want to turn into profit, but may never do so, you may want to consider burning that boat too. Take stock of all the boats in your life that you are dragging behind you which just need to be burned. You will start to see that there can be many things in life that may drag us down, slow our momentum, and even stall us on calm waters when we should be making extreme headway.

If your goal in your best decade is to move forward each day with love and courage, then you may need to burn some boats to ensure that happens.

Now, you are probably thinking, "*Ryan, I can't just cut things out of my life that easily. Some of my relationships are toxic. I need to do my job to pay my bills, etc.*" For you, that is a great first step. You have already acknowledged that you have boats in your life that need to be burned. We all have them. Some of us have less, others have more. So, here are my suggestions if you are having a hard time burning those boats which may be closer to home.

1. Try to lift up the other person if they are dragging you down. **We rise by lifting others, not by dragging them behind.** Keep others positive; keep them thinking about positive things in their lives, and encourage them to find their passions and hobbies while you continue to work on you within the relationship. If after a while, you find that this isn't working as you'd hoped, it may be easier to loosen the rope and allow that boat to drift a bit further from you. Bluntly put, distance yourself before you light it up.

2. If this does not work, you need to reel that boat back in and torch it. Move forward with your life and don't look back. This is the hardest step you can take, but it is sometimes the step needed for the other person(s) to see that they need to change as well.

Now, the above examples are boats that you may need to burn. What I want to show you now are examples of moments in your life when you simply need to burn the boats. If you are working a dead-end job, burning the boat applies. If your options for work are limited, try the best you can to push out of the "dead end" that you find yourself in. Try to find new ways of recreating yourself and your position within your job to make it less of a dead end for you.

> Do the best you can given what you have, where you have it, and whom you have it with.

Try to continue to add value to your position and think beyond the boat you are currently in. If all of this advice still doesn't work, burn that boat too. Life is incredibly short and staying in a dead-end job is not wise or helping anyone other than the bill collectors. Find a way to create a new opportunity by burning that boat. It's amazing, the things you can do when your back is against the wall.

It is not easy to just leave a job. Especially when you have family around you, mouths to feed, and bills to pay. If you are working a job over the summer to pay for school in the fall, I get that. Spend time trying to recreate yourself before you leave that particular job. You will likely discover something valuable that you can bring to a different area of work. Think about all of the emotional, physical, and mental energy you are spending each week in a job that gets you nowhere. What if you had those forty hours each week to recreate yourself, invest in a hobby, business venture, or spend more time with your family?

Some of the greatest entrepreneurs in history had to leave their jobs first. They had to burn boats to become truly invested in their ultimate dreams and ideas. Sometimes leaving our jobs gives us the push that we need to reach another level of potential. I touched on this in the first part of my book, but will also connect deeper with you on this in the next chapter.

Here's a story that will further prove my point. I knew a student who was only a term away from graduating from a very exclusive university program at a prestigious university. Before he finished his degree with one term to go, he decided to drop out and take his newly formed company to the next level. While his classmates were walking down the aisle to get their degree, he was signing a contract which would enable his company to become a leading brand. He had a choice: put all of his oars in the boat he built with his own hands, or stay in the other boat which may not have gotten him to his ultimate goal. Realizing the situation, he burned the "school boat" in order to invest in his "business boat." Smart choice given his circumstantial opportunity. The lesson I have taken from his story is this:

Oftentimes we become so invested in one path that we have to step back and evaluate if that is the path we really want to continue.

In those situations we may need to simply burn the boats. Here is another example. I had just started a job in Halifax, Nova Scotia and after working only two weeks, I received another offer to work full time in Edmonton, Alberta as a School Health Facilitator with a larger salary.

I had a huge choice to make.

I flew to Edmonton on the Monday following that weekend for the job interview. That afternoon, as I was reading a book in the city center while waiting for their decision, the call came through. We talked over the contract and I accepted the job, contingent on the fact that I start in two weeks. I jumped back on a plane, returned to Nova Scotia, gave my employer notice, and headed west in a matter of days. I had to burn some boats in a short period of time, but was cautious to not burn a bridge.

It was one of the best decisions I've made in my life. I remember saying on the plane to Halifax, "burn the boats, burn the boats." I knew what had to be done, but had to talk myself through it.

BRIDGES

This leads me to the second part of this chapter: burning bridges. You should try to avoid this in your best decade. Burning bridges is a term I use when ending something very badly. That something could be a serious relationship, a long standing job, or anything similar in magnitude, impact, and influence. Burning a bridge is never a good thing. You do *not* want to go through life making this a habit. In fact, you want to do this as little as possible.

So, how do you burn boats without burning bridges? I believe that an important lesson to learn early in your life is how you can burn a boat without burning a bridge along the way.

Let me explain.

First, let's understand why bridges are so important. We use them for walking across impassible depths of water, or for cycling over frozen terrain that would otherwise be disastrous. We use them to get us from one place to another. Some of us drive over bridges every day to and from work and don't even seem to notice. Bridges are often taken for granted.

I want you to think about how many bridges you cross each week to get your groceries, drive yourself somewhere for entertainment, or to take your kids to and from school. Whether these bridges are big or small, they all serve the same purpose:

> They safely and efficiently help us get from one place to another.

Let's imagine you get up tomorrow and that bridge you take automatically, every day is gone. How would you get to work?

Would it take you longer to get your kids to school?

Would traffic be crawling?

Would people be happy?

The same holds true for people and metaphorical bridges in our lives. Every relationship that you have with someone is a bridge out to the world and, more specifically, to *your* world. We have relational bridges, professional bridges, and spiritual bridges to name a few. All of these bridges are supported by important people that can help us move efficiently from one place to another in our best decade. The right people around us can be amazing bridges for our well-being. In my life, my father has been a huge bridge and support for me. Growing up, I always admired his love for my mother and how he treated her, respected her heart, and put others ahead of himself. In my mid-twenties as I was approaching my engagement, I needed affirmation of my heart's desire to marry the woman I love. So, I reached out to my dad over multiple phone conversations to hear his thoughts. After talking continuously for hours on one of my road trips, Dad asked me if I knew my answer. He had a funny way of allowing me to discover my own answers without him providing them for me. He is an incredible man who helped me bridge the gap from loving my girlfriend to marrying the woman of my dreams. I am very grateful for these conversations among the many other things my father has given me.

I have a good friend and mentor who has always been very supportive of my passion for wellness. When I first moved to Abu Dhabi; where he resides, he intentionally went out of his way to connect me with prospective employers so that I could broaden my professional horizon, build deeper relationships, and eventually open career options. He helped to open many doors which would help me go from where I was to where I wanted to be.

Educational bridges may be one of the most important bridges you can have in your teens, twenties, thirties and even forties and beyond. I have been blessed to have had about a dozen different educational bridges which have helped me get to where I am today. There were so many times in my late teens and early twenties where I was naive and full of energy and good intention. I didn't have much direction, but I had an ocean of ambition. Some of these educational bridges helped steer my ship straight, others challenged my bearings, while some even threw the anchor overboard so I could pause and reflect on where I was going. Whichever role they played in my life, I will forever be grateful for them. They know who they are.

I will, hopefully, build even more bridges in the next couple of years, should I continue to pursue the many opportunities that life has to offer. You too can have this.

Whether you like it or not, it is an art to be able to navigate life and reach your unlimited potential filled with joy and a strong sense of well-being without burning bridges, especially when you are young. If there is one thing Generation Z and millennials are able to do, it is burn bridges without truly knowing that they are doing so. Our parents, grandparents, and generations before them typically had smaller networks, and fewer connections. Yet they had stronger bridges which were nurtured through physical interactions or consistent telephone calls. Millennials and Generation X, on the other hand, have grown up surrounded by this thing called technology that provides us with two things:

First

An unprecedented ability to build bridges faster than ever before in human history. For example, we can snapchat, tweet, or instagram with our circles to constantly keep them current and important within our lives. Our capacity to build bridges rapidly without a geographical presence can be endless with social media communication platforms.

Second

Technology provides us with the opportunity to hide behind our screens to end a relationship, business arrangement, or 'loose end' without needing to ever see that person again. Do yourself a favor and don't hide behind your screen. Stand tall and stand by your decisions verbally and as physically as possible.

Social media, professional online networking, and instant messaging were all platforms that I was able to access, learn, and navigate effectively early in my twenties to help me become the most connected person I know in my field. (*Seriously, ask my wife, it drives her crazy*). This ability to navigate spaces in the palm of your hand with a smartphone is incredible. We have never had a higher capacity to build bridges in our lives than we do right now. I am not talking about selfies and Snapchat takeovers, I am talking about truly being able to intentionally connect anytime, anywhere, and in any way with those you want to build bridges with.

If you are in your best decade, you'd better be using your phone to your advantage. This is something I really dove into when I moved internationally for work. I was blessed enough to know a few friends at my school and in the city I was living prior to arriving, but in my specific field of health and wellness I knew virtually no one. This was a problem for me because I knew that to be successful I needed to be surrounded by like-minded leaders in my field. So, with the help of a great bridge builder and a small professional connecting website called LinkedIn, I got to work.

Within two weeks of arriving, I was setting up meetings, "cold calling" leaders via email, and inviting them out for coffee to connect personally with them. I reached out to about fifteen professionals on LinkedIn to meet for coffee and by the end of my second month I had met with about half of them to start developing deeper connections within my field. I cannot begin to tell you how valuable that mindset and decision making was for my future, because it is still being mapped out as a result of those coffee meetings. Use technology and social media to your advantage and start connecting with others to build bridges today. If you want more information on how to do this, read *Crushing It* by Gary Vaynerchuk.

I always find it funny connecting with leaders at the top of their fields. When I reach out to them it takes creative scheduling, but they are most always willing to meet and connect over a coffee. It's interesting, but most leaders at the top of their field are actually so highly respected that people don't reach out to connect with them.

When Donald Trump was first elected President of the United States, within about a month of being in office he reported that he 'felt lonely'. It is pretty lonely sometimes when you are at the top of your field, even though it shouldn't be! My point here is that you should not be afraid to reach out to connect with someone who you regard as a leader. They are people too. If they are great leaders they will be looking to broaden their network and influence by meeting with more people like you anyway. In your best decade, narrow in on a few influential leaders in your field and invite them out for a cup of coffee. Build a bridge that can make a huge difference in your life. Invest in knowing them now and you will see the benefits of this throughout your best decade.

On the opposite side of the coin, we have a tremendous opportunity never seen before in human history to let people down continuously and on our own terms. Our ability to build a bridge is just as great as our ability to burn a bridge through technology and social media. For example, there are certain conversations that need to be uncomfortable and are not solvable via text, instant message, or email. There are bridges that you need to physically and intentionally connect with from time to time before you begin asking favours from those bridges. You cannot walk across a bridge until it is fully built. Trust me on this one. I have seen this play out across multiple cultures, language barriers, and in different parts of the world. We all crave connectivity, relationships, and solid bridges regardless of who we are and where we come from.

In my life, I can count on one hand how many bridges I have burned and I specifically remember each one of them. There are four.

Why do I track this?

Because I have made it my life's mission to never be the topic of negative conversation at a family dinner table, business meeting, or phone conversation. Even though this is out of my control, I do think being intentional about it is important.

I am reaching my fourth decade of life, so I am ok with only having burned a few bridges along the way. In fact, that is almost one bridge burned per decade of life. If this isn't the case for you, no need to worry. You still have time to slow down and/or stop the burning today. Let me share another short story with you about a time I burned a bridge so that you do not make the same mistake that I did in your professional career.

There was a brief period of time when I was doing a lot of freelancing, contracting, and self-discovering. I got a call one day when I was out kayaking with one of my mentors, from an employer offering me a part-time position involving the marketing and selling of a sports nutrition brand in Canada. Don't worry, it wasn't one of those pyramid schemes. It was a bit different, but still something that I was on the fence about. As a professional in the wellness industry, I had never sold myself to the devil by selling and marketing a single sports supplement brand full time. However, for one reason or another, I took the position. At the time, I thought it would allow me to get closer to my goals, so I dove in.

To make a long story short, I didn't do very well in the position as I discovered that the product did not fully align with my values surrounding wellness and personal growth. I will spare some confidential details but for now let's focus on the bridge.

Knowing I was going to leave my position, I tried to find a candidate who had strong relationships in Atlantic Canada, who also lived a lifestyle of wellness and who could easily fill my position. After breaking news of my departure to my manager, I brought forward the information and strong recommendation for this individual to be my successor in the role.

Let's just say that my proposal was not well received. My manager did not approve of my leadership in that capacity, and the bridge lit up faster than the sky during the fireworks show celebrating Canada 150. I never ended up repairing that bridge. I moved on and took a few personal lessons from that experience that I carried with me to my next position and to my next leadership experience. I have made a personal effort since that time to remember the importance of keeping bridges sturdy while also building new bridges along the way. In reflecting, I probably should have deferred to their leadership advice first, before taking steps to bring in my replacement.

When should you leave a burned bridge behind, and when should you try to put that fire out to save what is left of the bridge? That is a great question to ask yourself if you haven't already. My advice would be this: if the bridge you burned was a professional bridge, leave that bridge behind and move on with your life.

The damage is done.

Jobs are replaceable, so it is best for both you and the organization to move forward.

If the bridge was a relational bridge, proceed with caution. Depending on how the bridge was burned, it may be salvageable or even rebuilt with care. People are emotional beings so you know best when, and if, you should try to reconnect with that person(s). The choice is yours. My advice would be to think clearly and deeply about this before you re-engage with that person. If you need additional support on this, send me an inbox tweet and I can talk you through this based on my experiences.

Some of you may be thinking, "*Ryan, how do I continue to build new bridges while also maintaining deep relationships with the bridges I have built in my career? In my personal life?*" The answer to this question, based on my experience, is quite simple. If you can go back to my chapter on "Living

With Intention" you will begin to answer those questions on building and sustaining relationships. The other biggest piece of advice I can give you is to continuously remember to stay connected with those around you both virtually and physically. Find conferences and events to attend where your former network will be. Reach out and reconnect with them via email to *genuinely* see how they are doing. If you continue to show them you want to invest in a life-long relationship with them, you will be able to keep communications open when future opportunities arise. Social media platforms such as Twitter, Facebook, and LinkedIn are inexpensive ways to keep these lines open. It sounds very simple, but do not become complacent with this ritual. People want to feel valued and they want to continue to know you. We all crave connection. Keep giving them the opportunity to connect long after they have helped you during a certain chapter of your life.

In your own life, you may now be reminded of an old friend or family member who built a lot of bridges for you early in your life and in your career. If you are in school, there is a good chance someone referred you to that school and helped build an educational bridge for you. If you are currently working, chances are someone has helped you along the way to obtain work in your current field. Yes, references can be great professional bridge builders for you! If you are to create your best decade, be intentional in reaching out to these people.

You may be reading this and thinking that you do not really have anyone around who is building bridges for you. If not, I encourage you to reach out to me and I will do my best to start connecting you with people in your field as soon as I can. Let me build a couple of bridges for you as you kick off your best decade.

In your own life, I want you to reflect on one time you burned a bridge and what that felt like.

How do you feel as you think about it?

How will it feel in the future?

Does the burning of this bridge leave a hole burned inside you?

In the following chapter, I will prepare you with strategies that will help you shift your mindset and your 'self stories' in order to move yourself forward. I will also share some thoughts on how powerful your stories can be once you have fully burned your boats.

CHAPTER 8
The Stories We Tell Ourselves

"Personal competence goes beyond words. It's a leader's ability to say it, plan it, and do it."
—John C. Maxwell

I will never complete a Spartan Race.
I will never run a marathon.
I will never be a professional athlete.
I will never have the house I want.
I will never be financially comfortable.
I am not good enough.
I will never find that Mr. or Mrs. Right.
I am not enough for my spouse.
I will never become the top associate in my company.

Do any of these statements resonate with you? Have you spoken any of these in your mind or out loud? If so, you are not alone. Many people underestimate their abilities and tell themselves daily that they are inadequate or not enough. Although many people believe that self doubt is on the decline, I believe that self-reporting of self doubt has increased. Many people struggle with self doubt although the signs now are different than what they were twenty years ago. I see self doubt manifest in the form of social media anxiety, lack of life focus, and resorting to self medication strategies such as various forms of binging (gaming, TV watching, internet use, etc.) You cannot live your best decade in this realm. Lack of confidence and self doubt have no place in your best decade.

To be quite honest, I wanted to leave this chapter out of the book. It was the hardest and most uncomfortable chapter to write, because it resonates with so many people who are struggling. The good news is, if you have read this far you are on your way to scaffolding your best decade and are ready for the added push to elevate your life. I am hopeful that you remain open as you allow me to guide you through your thinking so that you may reach a better state of well-being and internal fulfilment. You can bulletproof your mind now so that you become more positive, optimistic, resilient, and powerful as you approach a life of well-being in your best decade.

While attending university, I participated in a fundraiser collecting supplies for a school in Ghana. It was a movement-based event held at the university track. As a participant, you raised money by getting sponsored to run a specific distance or, alternatively, you could simply donate money without actively participating. At the time, I was working as a personal trainer part-time while finishing my Bachelor of Education degree.

During a session, while I was running with a client around the track, she challenged me to a task that I was almost unwilling to do. She said, "*Ryan, if you run sixty laps on the track during the fundraiser I will donate $2/lap to allow these children in Ghana to have school supplies.*" Now, sixty laps on a 400m track is the equivalent of running a half marathon, but I accepted the challenge as I knew it would be for a good cause. At this point in my life, I had only run the equivalent distance once, and at the time of the challenge I was only running short distances.

Photo: Anthony Williams (left), Wade Ball (Left Center), Captain Brendan O'Donovan (Right Center) and myself starting our "We Move This Town" fundraiser to raise money for a school in Ghana

On the day of the fundraiser I felt ready to run, but deep down I wasn't sure if it was possible to complete the proposed distance. I heard this voice in my head telling me that I couldn't do it and that I would fail my client and fail myself. Although I was feeding myself negative talk, I started running and ran the first few laps alongside friends (*fun fact - my future wife also ran in this fundraiser*). After a few laps my friends began to stop, but I continued along at my snail pace. I continued running until it became dark and began to rain.

As the rain fell, I ran and ran until I could almost no longer feel my hamstrings. I finally crossed the 400m start line at lap 60 and completed the challenge. There was one person there to greet me and that was my good friend and my eventual best man! I walked to his car, dove into the backseat because I could not bend my legs, and we headed for a kitchen party together. (*Yes, you read that correctly. Feel free to Google an East Coast kitchen party*).

I want to share another story with you about how easy it is to believe the stories we tell ourselves. In 2012, I had the opportunity to put a team together for the Terry Fox Run across the Confederation Bridge, which is the largest bridge built over freezing water which connects Prince Edward Island (PEI) to the rest of Canada.

The Terry Fox Run is an annual run held across Canada to raise money for Cancer treatment. Terry Fox was a mentally resilient Canadian who had a dream to live in a world that was cancer free. He set out to run across Canada after a cancerous tumor had resulted in the amputation of his right leg. He successfully ran from St. John's, Newfoundland, to Thunder Bay, Ontario before the cancer spread to his lungs and he was forced to stop running. (Source: http://www.terryfox.org/terrys-story/marathon-of-hope/). Cancer eventually overtook him, and his dream was turned into a lasting legacy which is still carried on today by many Canadians. Each year, Canadians celebrate Terry Fox and his vision by participating in the Terry Fox Run; however, the Confederation Bridge closes only once every five years specifically for the run.

Photo: My former colleague Jasmine and I running on the Confederation bridge during the 2012 Terry Fox Run for Hope.

That year, I took off with my team from St. Francis Xavier University to run from New Brunswick to PEI. The sunrise was incredible and the company was refreshing. Upon reaching PEI, with most of the team together, I realized that we had left the car in New Brunswick and now had to run back across the bridge. Another 13 km to go!

Logistically, I forgot that we should have parked on the PEI side prior to the run and shuttled over to New Brunswick before running towards our vehicle. I was exhausted as was most of my team, but we had no other option. So, we buckled down and started our return from the PEI side of the bridge back towards N.B. I honestly did not think we were going to make it as we had limited water and carbohydrates and the September sun was beaming down on us for what felt like hours. It was not ideal, and I began telling myself that I may not make it. I was really beginning to doubt myself when we approached the Canadian Military who were marching towards PEI. As we crossed paths, they saluted us for running back and doubling our distance. It was an engraving moment. I knew at that point that our best bet was to stick together, stay positive, and just put one foot in front of the other.

We finally made it back to our vehicle after hours of running across the North Atlantic. I will never forget that experience and I will never forget how happy I was to sit in a vehicle.

Photo: Me and my STFX University team taking a moment on the Confederation Bridge to admire the beautiful setting.

The point of both stories is this: sometimes we appear to know exactly what we are doing when we are doing it, but in reality we can be telling ourselves internally that we are not enough, that we cannot achieve our goals, and that we cannot succeed at the task at hand. We need to recognize these moments of self doubt in decision making, and those times during which we do not think we are enough to succeed. We need to acknowledge those thoughts and feelings, persevere, and overcome that thinking. As the famous writer Rudyard Kipling once stated in his poem "If", *"If you can greet triumph with disaster and treat those two imposters just the same… You will be a man, my son."* Life will make you create stories about yourself and your ability, but you do not have to listen to them. I specifically wrote about this in chapter one but it is worth repeating, "You do not have to listen to everything that you think"!

Nature follows the path of least resistance and in the 21st century almost everyone in a developed country lives a pretty carefree life. This can sometimes blind us from believing we can succeed, understanding the need to push boundaries, getting promotions over time, and even competing at a level of life we never thought possible. We all need to willingly step out, take a leap of faith, and truly invest in our core belief that we can meet our goals, that we can be the best on our team, or that we can get that promotion we have always wanted.

Instead of believing we can't do what we think we can, or basing our stories on what others decide those stories should be, I encourage you to take a leap of faith to invest in yourself and in your ability to live better in your best decade.

Think it and it can happen. Try it and fail forward. Test the water and then jump in whether it is frigid or steaming. Get dirty and get to work. Stop believing the stories that you are not enough, that you need to settle, or that you will only ever be as good as others think you are right now.

Your best decade is all about self definition, not public definition.

I want to take the time to share some tips on how to shift your mindset. I want you to begin uncovering the stories that you should be telling yourself, rather than continuing to believe the ones you are probably telling yourself now but shouldn't be. Here are a few changes you can make in your life as you begin to tell yourself new stories that will allow you to dream, stretch, and dive further into a life of fulfillment and well-being in your best decade:

1. **Affirmation** - I want you to take five minutes each day to tell yourself that you are desirable, that you are loved, and that you can do anything. You *can* achieve your goals and aspirations. Do this daily. Do not skip a day. Treat this time like a doctor's appointment. Would you miss your doctor's appointment? No, because you can rarely see the doctor when you really need to. This affirmation time should be on the same level of importance for you.

2. Journal - One of the best methods I have used to stay positive and to believe I can achieve my goals and visions is journaling. It is a valuable currency to invest in during your best decade. Making a habit of journaling

each day in your teens and twenties will pay dividends later in life. If you are not sure what to journal about, write a bit each day about how you feel, why you might feel the way you do, and what areas you are doing well in. I would also include some sentences about areas you feel you need to improve on.

3. **Network** - As a good mentor of mine once said, *"Ryan, I need to get away from Turkeys and surround myself with more Eagles."* After all, Turkeys are unable to fly, while Eagles soar high. We are products of our environment whether we want to believe it or not. If you can make a conscious effort in your best decade to surround yourself with Eagles, it will help you to reach your greatest potential in all capacity areas. If you can do this, you will soon find yourself flying high over the mountains with a greater confidence unlike any you have ever had before. Soar with Eagles!

4. Habits - We are a series of habits. Charles Duhigg has an amazing book on this called *The Power of Habit* (*see my book recommendations*). Each day, our decisions and our lifestyles are based on habits. I want you to step back and evaluate your habits. Are they helping you achieve the life you want? Are they producing results or are they just pure pleasure-based habits? Are they adding to your life or are they distracting you from reaching your dreams and goals? After you evaluate your habits, begin replacing *unproductive* habits with more *productive* habits. This could mean replacing a night out on the town with a night in reading a book and pre-planning your upcoming week. It could mean simply making sure you are spending your money on

high quality food to drive your wellness instead of spending your money on less trivial things.

5. **Move** - We live in the most sedentary time in human history. We sit instead of stand, we drive more than we walk, and we spend more time sitting in front of screens each week than whole cities of people did forty years ago. Get up, get your heart rate going, and get physically active. Find something that works for you and your lifestyle and make it a habit! Guard your movement time and treat it like a job. Find someone to keep you accountable and set S.M.A.R.T (*specific, measurable, achievable, realistic, targeted*) goals to keep you moving forward. If you are looking for more support email me at faheyconsulting@gmail.com and I will help you get started!

6. Focus - Get clear on who you are and where you are going. This is difficult for most of us, especially in our teens, twenties, and thirties in a world that constantly craves our curiosity. If focusing seems hard for you, keep all five steps I listed above on goal setting a priority in your life to help you focus more naturally. Try focusing in on a specific goal or a specific project and make it happen. Produce results and do not get distracted along the way. If your goal is to run a 5 km road race in twenty minutes, don't just start swimming in the pool to achieve this goal. Focus in on the goal, move forward with that goal, and focus on giving it your best shot. Do not sway in your focus either!

7. **Invest** - Robin Sharma, author of many great leadership resources and books, including *The Greatness Guide* and *The 5AM Club*, has said multiple times that the best

investment you can make is in yourself. I truly believe this. After all, there were multiple people who doubted I would ever author a book, yet here we are. I believe Robin is right. If you are able to go "all in" and invest in yourself and in your craft, do it! Invest on becoming better. Invest in learning more. Invest in that hobby you have always wanted to take from the back burner to the front, but never thought you could. Invest in your confidence to live the life you want with the people you want around you. Invest in becoming your best self now for the payoff later in life. This reminds me of a great quote by Loretta Claiborne who is a member of the International Special Olympics Board of Directors, which reads:

"Be your best. Look your best. Feel your best."

8. Sacrifice - "*Nothing good can stay gold.*" This was a quote from S.E Hinton's book *The Outsiders*, which I quoted during my valedictorian speech at my high school graduation. It has resonated with me ever since. ***If you want to shift your thinking and tell yourself stories that you should believe, you need to sacrifice something good to get something great.*** When you are young and all your friends are out partying and hitting every power hour they can find, you need to be mastering your self talk and self confidence behind closed doors. Turning down the good to become something great should be your ultimate goal. In your work life, when your colleagues are blowing their money on weekend bar visits, you need to be paying off any debts you may have, and investing in your future while building

a healthy lifestyle filled with rest, exercise, and hard work. In your forties and fifties you need to be invested in making yourself an example for your family, friends, and co-workers by building a greater reputation and influence within your peer groups. Let everyone around you know through your actions that *your* actions speak louder than words, and that you are invested in creating the best life for yourself and those around you. This will attract more high performing individuals to you which will attract more success over time. It is a compound effect. Compounding is a beautiful thing in your best decade!

9. **Narrate** - Telling the right story is one of the best ways to begin telling yourself (and others) stories that will change your world and enhance your well-being in your best decade. I want you to excavate the stories you have told yourself recently and put them in writing either in your journal or on your phone. I challenge you to commit to this and to be accountable by sharing it with someone you feel comfortable with. Let me help you get to the next level by sharing your story publicly.

10. Mentorship - Once you have practiced all nine of the above methods of transforming the way you communicate your own stories from negative to positive, it is time to seek out a trusted mentor. On my Twitter page, I have a list of mentors to help you get to where you want to be. Connect with me @wellnessrf so I can connect them with you! Alternatively, you may have someone in your life already that you trust to help guide you in the right direction, and who you feel will help you live your best life. If you are in your teens, I would encourage you to find a mentor in their forties,

fifties, or older to help share their insight and experiences with you. If you are in your twenties, I encourage you to find someone who has "walked the walk" to be your mentor. If you are in your thirties and forties, find someone who lives a similar life to you whom you admire, and who can help you get to the next level. No matter which stage of life you are in, do not force this process. Finding a mentor can be challenging, but is also very important for your personal development so that you may live your best life. If you are in your fifties and sixties, seek out a younger person whom *you* can mentor. Share your wealth of knowledge and experience with them.

My hope is that the above strategies will help you begin to shape new stories about yourself to help you reach new heights and pursue a life of well being in your best decade as you reshape your narrative. It takes work, dedication, and loads of resilience to build a life that is rich and provides you with a sense of well-being, fulfillment, and purpose. It is not easy and there are no quick fixes to launching yourself on a trajectory of success and unlimited potential. You need to put the above practices in place each day of your life from here on out, in order to become the person you want to become and to see the eventual results spill into your life.

I mentioned earlier in this chapter that this was one of the hardest to write because it hits close to home for all of us one way or another. I used to believe the negative stories I told myself, until one day I woke up and realized that I was capable of so much more. It is time for you to stand up and do the same in your own life. The amazing thing about our lives is that we have the ability each day when we wake up to create a new story. Recreate daily. We can become something greater than we were just one day before. What a blessing. The best decades are in front of you so do not waste any more time believing your current, yet old, stories. Generate fresh new stories and move forward with drive, passion, vigor, purpose, focus, and poise.

Life is short and time is precious.

Start now!

Write a new story about how you began to author the best decade of your life!

CHAPTER 9
Abandon The Comfort Zone

> *"There is tremendous growth on the cliff of your comfort zone where fear and uncertainty play together."*

THIS MAY VERY well be the hardest chapter for you. This chapter should challenge you. Before I dive too much into comfort zone thinking, I want you to take a moment to reflect on where you are most comfortable right now in your life. Let's start by talking about the 'Big Three' areas I introduced earlier - *professionally, relationally* and *personally*. For example, If you are comfortable in your current profession, write that down and include the aspects of comfort that you enjoy within your job. If you are comfortable in your current relationship, write down specifically what is comfortable about that relationship. If you are comfortable with where you are at in your personal life, write down why you are comfortable with this.

Try to identify the many aspects within each area that make your life comfortable. There are blank pages at the end of this book if you need some additional space to reflect on your comfort zone.

Professionally:

Relationally:

Personally:

There are more areas than those I have listed above, but I want to park your thinking here for a moment. Let's now dive into comfort zone thinking. If you have a pulse, you have a comfort zone. I cannot put it any simpler than that. Some of us have broad zones and constantly challenge the fringe areas of our lives. Others have narrow zones, and challenge only selected areas within themselves. Finally, there are those who are unaware of where their boundary lies. This is a powerful analysis for you to do!

Truth is, a lot of us go through life not fully understanding the boundaries of our comfort zones. In our teens we feel immortal, in our twenties we think we are unstoppable and in our forties, we can easily take our comfort zones for granted by resorting to the 'safe' decisions that never push us beyond the status quo.

I recently had a conversation with a dear friend of mine and it nearly broke my heart. She was talking to me about my insane ability to embark on new adventures, to challenge my comfort zone, and to just 'do' things as I learn the 'how' along the way. She then insisted that she lives vicariously through me because she did not travel when she had the chance earlier in her career. I wanted to challenge her to push her personal comfort zone and limits to create an experience for her family like no other. So I gave her some passionate words to consider: it is never too late to push the boundaries of your own comfort zone, or the comfort zone of someone else.

A powerful thought on comfort zones is that they become more rigid as we go through life. I am not really sure why this is, but as children we are curious, mischievous, and ambitious. As we get older these traits are replaced by a heightened need for security, prosperity, and safety.

I absolutely love the quote at the end of the final *Lord of The Rings* movie when the well-aged Bilbo Baggins recognizes the ship and observes the sunset to which he would sail towards. When asked if he was ready to sail, his response was, "*I believe I am ready for another adventure.*" You are never too old to push the boundaries and to venture into the unknown.

In the last chapter, I talked about the stories we tell ourselves and I challenged you to ***change your story***. Recreating the next twenty four hours as they come and thinking big picture are two ways to change your story. This holds true for your comfort zone as well.

In November of 2015, I was honored to be asked to present to important leaders in education at a conference in Edmonton, Alberta. This was uncharted territory for me. Prior to this, I had only ever presented to teachers and principals. District leaders were a whole new ball game. The morning of the presentation, I knew my comfort zone was going to expand. I was nervous, anxious, and even happily stressed about what I was prepared to deliver. All signs of challenging my professional comfort zone. I stepped up to the plate and knocked it out of the park. The presentation went so well that it snowballed into a long-lasting relationship with the leadership of the largest geographical school district in Alberta. This would not have happened had I not challenged my comfort zone.

What I find most interesting about comfort zones is that they truly are 'zones'. For example, depending on the day, the zone could be larger or smaller than the day before. Zones can change. Anyone who has ever had to go to work while feeling sick knows exactly what I mean here. On days when just getting to work is the goal, you are much less likely to challenge leadership, innovate greater products, or smile while you engage with your team in the staff room.

Your 'zone' is very small and your bed is the only thing that you need for comfort.

On other days you may feel inspired, fired up, and lit with passion. You are on top of the world and if someone asked you to skydive, you may actually entertain the idea. You know what those days feel like. If you haven't had one of these in a while, it is time to take everything you have learned so far in this book to make those days happen as you create the best decade of your life.

The bottom line here is that comfort zones are not fixed. We make ourselves believe they are fixed. They have variance, they change, expand and contract with our day to day life. Since this is the case, I want to challenge you to push the boundaries of your current comfort zone. Act now and create a more fulfilling life that is rich and abundant for you. Let me show you how.

Below is a decision-making process for challenging your comfort zone. Ask yourself these important questions to evaluate if you are truly challenging your comfort zones:

1. Will this decision challenge me? In what way(s)?

2. Is this decision risky or hazardous? (Risk is good, hazardous is not)

3. How will I grow from this decision? (Think of the 'Big Three')

4. What is truly holding me back from making this decision?

On August 30th, 2017, I remember standing in the Edmonton airport, bags in hand, freaking out. I was pacing, sweating and trying to find calmness. The decision I had made to leave my partner, family, career, and assets, and throw conventional thinking out the window to travel to Abu Dhabi for a teaching gig hit me hard. I was anxious, nervous, and stressed all at the same time. What if I was making a huge mistake? What if my partner and I grow apart in the months to come? What if I hate my new life in the UAE? What if I die? Having never lived and worked anywhere outside of North America, I was understandably overwhelmed.

Comfort zone - challenged!

So, what did I do? I recognized this anxiety and called my family as fast as I could. I could not get ahold of my parents, so I called my partner's mother. It was as though the stars aligned for that conversation. Her sense of calm and her empathetic heart allowed me to share how I was feeling. She gave me words of encouragement and prayed for me over the phone. She reassured me of the decision we had made and she relaxed my, then, anxious heart. That conversation changed my day and I am truly grateful that she was home to take my call!

Following this conversation, I called my family who finally answered the phone. They were relaxing at home with their phones on silent, therefore, missing my persistent attempts to get ahold of them. Here I was in panic mode only moments earlier, and they were just having a casual day at the house. We talked for a bit and my Dad distracted me with some thought-provoking questions which I was also really grateful for! I became more calm, focused, and ready to take the leap with faith. I was ready to burn the boats!

The reason I tell you this story is because I want you to know that it is not easy to abandon the comfort zone. Our zones protect us at times. They are there so that we survive. We are designed to survive and assess 'risks'; to follow the path of least resistance with the least amount of danger to ourselves. It is basic human nature. However, I also want to tell you that there are times in life when you simply must toss all that feels comfortable out the window to create a life worth living that is waiting for you just on the other side of fear. In your teens this may mean traveling internationally, working for a great organization like Habitat for Humanity, or doing a high school exchange with a school in a different country. I can tell you this because I am living proof of it. I wrote this chapter while sitting in 37 degree Celsius weather on Saadiyat Beach in the UAE with one of my mentors. I took my own advice and am now sharing it with you.

In your twenties, going outside your comfort zone may involve creating a startup or pursuing your post-secondary education. It may look like starting one university degree, only to change your program of study before completion.

Call the audible.
Challenge the comfort zone.
Get to work.

In your thirties, moving beyond the boundaries of your comfort zone may mean moving your family to a new city for a fresh start. It may also mean selling your home and moving into a tiny home to allow you to vacation with your family more often. ***Call the audible, make aggressive yet calculated decisions, and don't regret the action.*** Also, as Tony Robbins would say, "Make the decision and don't look back!"

Another interesting aspect of comfort zones, is that if you consistently challenge them you are in for a rich and fulfilling life. Some of the best moments in my life were discovered at the edge of my comfort zone. They revealed pieces of me that I didn't know existed. I found parts of me that I would not have found otherwise. ***Let your best decade be a complete unveiling of who you are.***

Perfect example: in November of 2013, I took a road trip across America and planned to run my first Spartan Race in Milwaukee, Wisconsin. I had never run one of these races before, but I was scheduled to be at a conference in Milwaukee anyway so I thought, why not?

Let me first say, the people of Wisconsin are some of the most amazing people I have ever met. The Physical Education Specialists there work hard and endure harsh winters with warm hearts filled with fondness for their students. A lot like kind-hearted Canadians: they are resilient, resourceful, loving people.

I made it to Milwaukee the morning of the race, and I am pretty sure it was the first day of winter in Wisconsin. Jeez, it was cold! The race was held at Miller Park and was part of the Spartan Stadium Series which are completed in a Major League Baseball Park. It was incredible and it was cold. At the start line, I met a great man from Indiana who worked for his dad's paper company there. It was also his first race, so we decided to run together. He pushed me, and I pushed him. We talked and laughed and shared stories as we competed together. We finished in the top 20% of participants in our field and celebrated our accomplishment together over a classic American donut. We came, we met, we conquered. I love how racing brings people together. What a beauty!

What I didn't tell you is that I had to drive from Milwaukee to Windsor, Ontario after the race to meet up with my friend who was living there. I left my medal around my neck and, with my compression socks still on, I drove as fast as I could around Lake Michigan. I had never made that drive before and it was the longest leg of my three-week road trip. I was tired, anxious, alone, and I was uncomfortable. Comfort zone - challenged! Miraculously, I made it to my friend's place just after midnight. I was never so happy to see a familiar face.

In those thirty hours, I felt I had achieved a tremendous amount of growth and confidence. I had finished a race in the top 20% of my field, drove across two states, and somehow made it to Canada with energy to spare. Ask me if I would do it again. Heck, Yes!

I heard Comedian Amy Schumer say once that hiking isn't really hiking if you can bring Starbucks and a pita. The same holds true of your comfort zone. You need to do more than just say you are going to challenge your comfort zone. ***You need to turn thoughts into words, words into action, and action into results***. All on the edge of your comfort zone. If you can get to that edge you'll see that life is rich, fulfilling, beautiful, and wonderful out there.

Here is a small diagram which may reflect your current life. Each time you challenge your comfort zone it can grow bigger and bigger. Each time you turn away from challenging your comfort zone it becomes smaller and smaller. Think of it as a muscle. If you work your muscles strenuously over time, they will grow stronger and bigger. If you don't, you will experience muscular atrophy and become weaker.

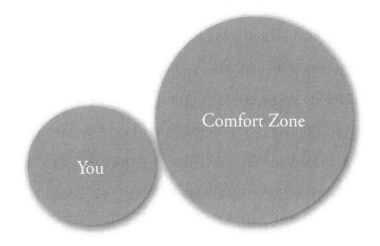

Each of us is on our own individual journey through life. I cannot define your comfort zone for you. It is an assessment that only you and, if applicable, your partner can make. You are the master of your destiny, the captain of your rich and fulfilling life. It is your compass to navigate, and navigating wisely is important.

Chapter 9: Abandon The Comfort Zone

Photo: Me, admiring the sunset on a desert safari in the UAE.

At the beginning of this chapter, I got you to write down all of the areas in which you are comfortable. Now, I want you to flip back to what you wrote down. Take the stories I have told you and commit to challenging the areas of your life that you are most comfortable in. For example, if you are comfortable relationally, maybe you are beginning to take your partner for granted. Maybe it is time to do something crazy and daring together to liven up your life and/or your relationship.

If you are comfortable professionally, ask for a leave to travel or to put energy into something that challenges your comfort zone. This could even be a hobby of yours. Or maybe, you straight up change jobs. Make something happen not just for the sake of making something happen, but because you believe it challenges you! If you are comfortable physically, try running a road race or signing up for a physical competition that will push your limits. Complete some tangible actions that will allow you to expand your current comfort zone in different areas of your life. There is an incredibly rich life on the other side, and I can't wait for you to tell me about it.

Now I want you to lay out some specific action items on how you are going to challenge your comfort zone in each of these areas of your life.

Professionally:

Relationally:

Physically:

Spiritually:

Intellectually:

Mentally:

Socially:

Emotionally:

Your list here may be small or large and each area may have a different range of items. The goal here is to have at least one action item in each area of your life. The most important thing is to not overwhelm yourself. Now I want you to go back and assign timelines to specific action items to accelerate your growth and create your best decade.

This is not a solo discovery. Once you have set reasonable timelines, I want you to call or email a friend to hold you accountable to your action items. *There is no greater force for challenging you than having an accountability partner who loves you and respects you.*

If you do not have that person, simply connect with me at faheyconsulting@gmail.com and I will help hold you accountable in creating the best decade of your life by abandoning your comfort zone while you plunge in and discover new territories. Going alone means you will probably go quickly. Going together means you will go far, quickly.

CHAPTER 10
The Yes/No Equation

> *"Half of the troubles of this life can be traced to saying yes too quickly and not saying no soon enough."*
>
> —Timothy Ferriss,
> *The 4-Hour Workweek*

Powerful thought (PT):

Respectfully saying no is a crucial concept for you to understand in your best decade.

I MET WITH A leader at New York University on the Abu Dhabi Campus in the fall of 2017. We conversed for a while before we landed on the topic of time-takers and the fact that if you invest time and money into yourself now, it will pay dividends to you in the future. With that investment, you sometimes have to respectfully say no to others. I am so thankful that this gentleman validated my thinking.

Another PT:

Everything you say 'yes' to decreases your capacity to say yes to something else.

Simply put, if you say yes to one thing, you are likely saying no to something else. I wrote a blog a few years ago on the energy management equation. The equation stated that our world thinks more about time management than it does about energy management. We often feel that we do not have enough time. However, I want you to consider this: do we have enough energy to execute our day-to-day and week-to-week tasks? We all run short on time even though we all have equal amounts of it each day; therefore, I believe it is an energy conversation rather than a time conversation.

This is why I want to talk to you about the yes/no equation. You only have so much energy to expend in one day. There are only so many things you can say yes to before you have to start entertaining the "no". Let me tell you a great story about this real-life equation.

When I moved to Abu Dhabi, I made a clear goal to provide myself with a more balanced life by saying "no" more than I said "yes" in the run of the week. The first week of my 2017/18 school year, my school's administration was encouraging all teachers to sign up for at least two professional development committees within the institution. Having put much energy into speaking with teachers about staff wellness just a semester before while living in Edmonton, Alberta, I knew I should probably hold back from overcommitting too early. But, of course, I said yes to two committees before being told I was also on a third.

It was not wise.

On top of this commitment, I was also diving into my coaching position as the schools' football season was fast approaching. I immediately felt overwhelmed. This was only my first week. Everything I instructed teachers just a semester ago to avoid, I was now doing. I was not taking my own advice. So, I made a personal decision during my second week of teaching to manage my time and energy more effectively. I realized that although I wanted to coach multiple sports throughout the year, football would be my only sport. I needed the downtime to focus on my goals and dreams, as well as to invest more time in my partner, our relationship, and our life outside of work. Saying no to other coaching opportunities meant I could say yes to quality time with the woman I loved.

For most of us, saying "yes" is so easy. Many people tend to overcommit, under deliver, and, as a result, get stuck in a cycle that becomes a lose/lose situation for them. Perfect example: so many educators get asked to be on committee XX and XY. Once they say yes, they often find out a month later that the curriculum is changing and they must overhaul their teaching. Many attend a few professional development sessions and then have to teach their colleagues what they have learned outside of school hours. Saying yes to all of that leadership, means saying no to a quality personal life. I see it all too often, which is why so many educators are burning out and leaving the profession in herds. Committees, meetings, and superfluous activities that solve trivial, non-urgent problems are time-takers. This is true in any profession. Let me explain a bit more about this.

"Time-takers" is a term I like to use when referring to those things in our professional, relational, and personal lives that simply suck valuable time and energy from us each day and leave us with little to fill our capacity jars. Better yet, they take time away from truly focusing on our goals within the "Big Three" areas of our lives. Common time-takers holding you back from your best decade include:

Relational Time-Takers

1. **Social Media (SM):** This one is bigger than most people give it credit. Social media can take time away from an intimate relationship that you never get back. Invest quality time! Don't waste it! Draw your boundaries. Say no to SM and yes to your relationships. Be more than just a decent and distracted person. Be fully present in reality.

2. **Texting:** I love the book *Everyone Communicates, Few Connect* by Author John C. Maxwell. He writes that so many people *communicate* in our world, but very few know how to actually *connect*. Put the phone down and take time back by investing minutes into a *quality* conversation and quality connection.

3. **Dishes:** Only if done alone. If done with a significant other, this can be a time for bonding and conversing. This is a conditional time-taker.

4. **Overcommitment:** Overcommitting to hobbies, sports, extracurriculars, etc., will leave you with very little time to invest in your significant other. Be mindful of this

before you sign up for something that will make you say "no" to your most intimate relationships.

5. **Fantasy**: I used to be a hardcore fantasy football subscriber. If I was still 'playing' fantasy football, I would not have written this book. Why? Because my mind would have been consumed with trivial thoughts about whether my quarterback was going to throw an interception in the fourth quarter or not. As a matter of fact, when I started dating I called the fantasy group I was involved with and told them I wouldn't be participating in any more fantasy football. They asked, "*Why Ryan? We need you!*." My answer, "*I want Sundays to be reserved for quality time with my partner.*" Get quality time back!

PT:

Redefine your time; redefine your prime.

PROFESSIONAL TIME-TAKERS

6. Meetings: There is nothing I hate more than inefficient and under-productive meetings. I would like to know the number of minutes per year that people have lost collectively due to small talk and trivial agenda items at meetings. A good friend of mine told me that he now institutes thirty eight minute meetings at his work. That leaves twenty two minutes following the meeting for a washroom break and time to make any phone

calls before entering the next meeting at the top of the hour. Brilliant.

7. **Email**: Tim Ferriss is all about checking emails once a day and I genuinely think he is on to something. While I was living and working in Alberta, I remember being on email until 10:00 pm, only to wake up the next day to repeat the same thing after regular working hours. This can evolve into a time-taker beast! The country of France recently passed a law that forbids employers to email employees after 7:00 pm in the evenings and before 7:00 am in the mornings. We need less email and more time for pure connection in our best decade, so limit this time-taker.

8. Ego: This is such a time-taker, and it often goes unnoticed. I have seen so many people try to climb to the top early in their career who seem to have forgotten the meaning of life. **Vocation is part of life, vocation is not life.** All of their time is consumed by their work. Many wake up one day realizing that it should have been less them, more others. My grandfather died before I was born, but one quote he passed down was this, "*I would rather die owing a million, than having a million.*" Unless you want to die being buried with hoards of unspent money, redefine your time and outlook on your life as well as your success. Redefine your priorities.

9. **Superfluous Work**: I love the scene in *Office Space* when all of Ron's supervisors come by his desk asking for the updated 'TPS Report'. It leaves you wondering, what is a TPS Report and why do so many people need it so quickly? Ron becomes very frustrated and anxious

because he cannot complete his TPS Report correctly as multiple supervisors want it done differently. Superfluous and inefficient work in the 21st-century job force and in education kill productivity and take time. Don't add layers of trivial work.

10. Mixing Up Urgent and Important: This is a sneaky time-taker in your best decade. Too often I see businesses and organizations experience fatigue and burnout because they don't know how to distinguish between urgent and important (*for more information on this concept, read "The 7 Habits of Highly Effective People" by Stephen Covey*).

For example: While it is important for you to provide clear instruction to your students about how to use a playground, it is more urgent to give your attention to a safety concern on the playground, such as an exposed nail or a loose board. In your own life, take some time to think about when the 'urgent' and 'important' tasks can get murky. Identify that space and think clearly about the differences between the two and how you can better identify these differences as you roll through your best decade. This will be key for reducing stress and making better decisions in your best decade.

Here is another example: I love when keynote presenters get up in front of a crowd and freak out thirty minutes before their presentation because something technical doesn't work properly. Ever notice how the presenter is typically stressed, yet the 'tech guy' is as cool as a cucumber? Why? Because it is his job to live in the important matrix, not the urgent. What is urgent for the presenter is not urgent for the tech guy who is not the person presenting. Don't mix up the difference between urgent and important.

Personal Time-Takers

11. **Streaming**: One of the biggest time-takers I have noticed, is our society's obsession with Netflix and other streaming platforms. We live in a consumer society that has conditioned us to constantly consume many types of content. We are consumers of shows, movies, food, etc. Although we are master consumers, living a life without Netflix or Crave TV in your best decade is possible. I still do not have a Netflix account. Yes, I do stream from time to time when my partner wants me to watch a show with her. And yes, I do use my sister's account (*Thanks, Megan!*). But life is about balance, and spending the majority of your free time streaming movies and TV shows can easily throw off your balance by taking valuable time away from you, which could have been spent on more productive activities. Do yourself a favor and choose an hour of walking or a thirty minute run instead of that third or fourth episode on Netflix. It will change your life and leave you far more fulfilled.

12. **People**: We are all a by-product of our environments. People can be one of the biggest and toughest time-takers to talk about. As you read this you may already be thinking about some people in your life who just take time away from you. You may be carrying

their emotional baggage, helping them through every step of life, or simply not allowing yourself to let them go so that you can free up some time to sort out your own needs. On the inverse, you may have someone in your life who pushes you to become great in multiple capacity areas. Instead of these folks being time-takers, they are time-creators. My good friend and mentor Matt MacDonald is one of those people in my life who pushes me to be the best version of myself in blowing the lids off of my capacity jars. We all need people in our lives to thrust us forward, especially with regard to areas like our physical fitness. Personal trainers need personal trainers, and students need quality educators who lead by example and encourage them to move through quality programming. Nature follows the path of least resistance, but I encourage you *not* to accept that law, even if it feels natural. Adapt, grow, and push your physical fitness with those around you who help keep you motivated and elevate your game. Let these people help you reach your best decade in all areas by giving you the gift of their time which creates a healthier, more productive life for you in your best decade.

13. **No Goals:** Our lives ebb and flow. For instance, in my life I have a Spartan season, academic season, contracting and speaking season, and a rejuvenation season. Although I will admit I need to spend more time in the rejuvenation season, what keeps me balanced, productive, effective and healthy in all areas of my life? Goal setting. A few years ago in my early twenties, I was all over the map. I was disorganized, could not maintain healthy relationships with others,

and did not have consistent fitness levels. In short, my life was not balanced. I did not have proper goals that helped keep me on track and living the life that I wanted to live. Setting goals was the magic ingredient missing in my "best decade recipe". All of this began to change when I started creating spreadsheets on my iPad using the Numbers App. I organized my passions, priorities, goals, ambitions, relationships, and hobbies so that I could enter this space weekly and check in on my progress in each of these areas. It was the key habit that took me from "dream-making" to "dream-taking". It allowed me to see success when I needed a pickup. I was able to see my fitness cycles and assess my fitness periodically. It also allowed me to be comfortable with my level of fitness as I progressed through different seasons of my life. It was brilliant. For you, this may be journaling, recording voice notes on your phone, or simply using a calendar on your fridge. Either way, you must set, assess, and reset goals if you are to sustain balance in your best decade.

14. **Traffic:** Getting stuck in traffic is annoying at best. You can make the most of this time by listening to your favorite podcast but, ultimately, no matter which way you look at it, being stuck in traffic is a time-taker. This one is tricky, because no one ever signs up to waste time in traffic and yet it still happens every day. One method I used to reduce time spent in traffic, while living in one of the fastest growing cities in Canada, was taking side streets and backroads. I also made a conscious effort to go to work early, so I could leave earlier to avoid congestion. This decreased my time in

traffic which allowed me to say 'yes' to more productive time in the office while all was quiet!

15. **Lines:** I love Black Friday. What an excuse to waste time standing in long lines to spend money you don't have. Two words...Time-Taker. Avoid lines whenever you can, especially during Black Friday!

16. **Video Games:** When I started my first teaching practicum in Trenton, Nova Scotia, I remember asking one of my grade seven students one day, "*What do you do with all your time after school each day?*" His response, "*Video games. I play video games every night until at least midnight.*" It was appalling. Video games are a huge time-taker for him and he didn't realize it. Saying yes to hours and hours of video gaming, meant that he was saying no to good health, healthy socialization, stronger emotional well-being, and positive mental health.

The best decision I ever made was selling my video game system during my freshman year at St.FX University to pay for an additional course. It allowed me to start making better choices with my downtime by saying "yes" to things like blogging, socializing, building a business, and engaging in physical activity.

Time-takers are also why many dieting adventures actually fail. All of the things listed above take valuable time away from us and our eating habits are the first to be affected.

It is important to note that not all time-takers are bad or created equal. For example, you may really enjoy time spent on any number of these time-takers, and you may only work twenty hours a week, but perhaps your job requires a ton of mental energy. If so, this may cause you to feel tired during your week which means you need to take time to rest and may need to take daily naps. This is not a bad thing, as long as those naps are powering you to stay focused on your goals.

Other time-takers can also be beneficial. Things like hobbies, books, exercise, etc. For example, I have spent countless hours writing this book. Is that a waste of time? Absolutely not! It is a time-taker that aligns with my goals and values. It has enabled me to create and navigate my best decade and beyond with my family whom I cherish. Find the good time-takers (*ones that align with your values*) and evaluate them just as you recognize and evaluate the negative time-takers in your life.

If you are struggling to wrap your head around how this looks for you, I want you to do something for yourself right now. I would like for you to clear your mind of obligations, turn off your smartphone, and focus on writing down the top five time-takers in your typical week. These time-takers may be things you wish to increase, or they might need to be reduced and/or eliminated altogether. Once you have these written down, determine which, if any, are eating into time you dedicate to your goals and values. Could you have achieved and/or developed these earlier through living with intention?

Now, I want you to circle the time-takers that do not directly align with your goals and values. If they miraculously all align, then great. Keep saying yes to those things as they are not only important to you, but also your future. However, if you are like many people doing this exercise right now, you may notice that you have circled at least one to two of your time-takers, which you have determined do not align with your goals and values. That is ok. Recognition is the first step, but keep in mind that, recognition without action is a false start. False starts can only go so long before they disqualify you from the race towards your best decade. So, I want you to take the next page of the book to write out some ideas and strategies that you can build into your week to reduce or even eliminate those non-productive time-takers. By doing this, you are making room to say YES to things that will allow you to go from good to great. Life is rich and full of enough opportunity for us to live a fulfilling life if we are able to use our time more wisely along the way.

Goals and Values:

1.

2.

3.

4.

5.

Time-Takers (*things that are preventing you from reaching your goals and taking time away from your "Big Three"*):

Relational (Rel)

1.

2.

3.

Professional (Pro)

1.

2.

3.

Physical (Phy)

1.

2.

3.

Personal (Per)

1.

2.

3.

Ideas can change the world. Ideas can also change *your* world. What are some ideas you are thinking about which can help you reduce or eliminate non-productive time-takers from your life? Who are some individuals that you need to add to your best decade to increase your capacity, health and production in your big three? Feel free to map these out, draw them out, or scribble some notes below.

Ideas:

Some strategies to eliminate time-takers are actually quite easy to think about. Particularly, some that I have used in my own life include:

1. Removed data plan from my phone (Phy)
2. Restructured my morning routine (Phy, Per)
3. Scheduled date night with my partner (Rel, Per)
4. Read and meditated before bed (Per)
5. Limited my Netflix use (Phy)
6. Set aside a budget for new books (Per)
7. Prepared my food for the week (Per)
8. Created all tweets only once a month using Hootsuite (Pro)
9. Surrounded myself with more like-minded people (Phy, Pro)
10. Allotted 1 day per week to read and reflect at the beach, in that season (Per)
11. Said no to coaching additional sport teams at my school (Pro)
12. Chose active transportation over driving (Phy, Per)
13. Streamlined my banking: reduced my number of credit cards and cash flow (Per)

Now, I want you to develop some specific strategies for how you plan to reduce or eliminate time-takers from your weeks. Feel free to use any of mine as a launching point or to email me at faheyconsulting@gmail.com if you are stuck and need help developing specific strategies that will work for you.

Strategies to reduce and/or eliminate time-takers each week:

1.

2.

3.

4.

Now I want you to shift gears to thinking more about time-creators which I referred to earlier. Time-creators are individuals who seem to multiply your time by adding value to your best decade in multiple capacity areas. Take a moment to list out some individuals who are currently serving that role in your life. If you don't have anyone serving that role, brainstorm some individuals who can become a time-creator for you in your best decade.

Time-Creators (*People that are lifting and thrusting you to reach or exceed your goals and adding to your capacity jars as they relate to the "Big Three"*):

1.

2.

3.

4.

Once you have your list of about 3-4 individuals, I would encourage you to begin reaching out to them to connect for a walk, a great cup of coffee or just to connect via Skype. This will be crucial in the creation and follow through of your best decade.

I want to leave you with some final bits of advice before we move on. Learn to say "no" in your best decade. This is a powerful skill to master early in your life. If you are reading this and are later in life, that is ok too. It is still just as vital to learn this skill now, and to approach your days by focussing clearly on your values.

Far too often, I see people overcommit and underdeliver on their week-to-week tasks because they have stretched themselves too thin. I am guilty of this at times myself. Do not do this to yourself. Play hardball with your time and throw elbows for personal time off by learning to say no. Put into practice the idea of honing in on your goals and values and that will allow you to say no with confidence and clarity. Hang your hat on your goals and values and do not let anyone tell you your values should be different.

They are yours.

Own them!

When I was writing this book, I was asked to go out multiple times with friends but I said no repeatedly until this book was finished. When people asked me why I was not going out and "having fun", I confidently responded that I wanted to stay in to crush my goals and write my book. That was a goal of mine and saying no with confidence and clarity allowed me not to waver in my response. People can take offense if you turn them down, but they will get over it. Reminding them why you are choosing option B over option A with them, is both wise and respectful. This will gain you respect and not burn any bridges as you continue to crush your goals while also defending your time.

I want to end this chapter with three more PT's to help you build your best decade:

1. *Learn to say no to the right things now, in order to allow yourself to say yes to the right things later.*
2. *Entertain the no. Get comfortable with welcoming it.*
3. *Redefine your time; redefine your prime.*

CHAPTER 11
The Hungriest Person In The Room

> *"Champions aren't made in the ring, they are merely recognized there."*
>
> —*Joe Frazier,*
> *World Champion Heavyweight Boxer*

YOU WILL BE different after you read this chapter. Buckle up.

It doesn't matter if you are in a position of leadership or not, this chapter will change your life and it will change the way you look at the world around you in your best decade.

It is time for you to think big about your life. In chapter eight, you challenged your comfort zone in many areas, and I hope you gained some powerful ways you can expand your comfort zone. Now, I want you to become the hungriest person in the room.

Wait. What?

Yes. I want you to become the hungriest person you know. If you want to live a life that is rich and fulfilling by creating your best decade, you need to become the hungriest person in the room.

Photo: Being hungry. Picking big things up and putting them down outside my former school in Oxford, NS.

Tenth grade was a big year for me. I realized something that changed my life. I realized that I was never going to be an amazing math student. I realized that I would only ever be somewhere in the middle of the class.

That same year I became a very dedicated runner. I also realized that because I have abnormally flat, wide feet, with a large gap between my first and second toes, I would never become an elite, high performance runner. Anatomically I was not built for the job. However, I decided I would give it my best shot and invest 100% of myself in athletics and in my education to see where I would land.

Despite working twice as hard in math to remain in the middle of the class, two years later I was elected Valedictorian by my student peers, and was one of two gentlemen in my class to graduate with honours. I was very proud to represent my class and to inspire my fellow grads to lead with courage, honour, and integrity as they ventured out into the world. I left them with this modified quote from S.E Hinton's book, *The Outsiders:* "*Stay gold grads of 2007. Stay gold.*" This reigns true for me today and, hopefully, remains in the hearts of those I had the privilege to address that day.

While I was a freshman at St. Francis Xavier University I also had a wake up call, which was more challenging than the one I experienced in tenth grade. I was failing chemistry and, even after hiring a tutor, realized that I wasn't cut out for the subject. For the first time in my academic life, I dropped out of a course. It was a defining moment for me. I felt like a failure for the first time in my life. I came home at Thanksgiving during my freshman year with a low sixties average in all of my courses. Thinking back to the resilience I built in high school, I decided I would work twice as hard and become better. By the end of my freshman year, I had pushed that average into the high seventies. For me, it was progress, and progress equaled success, so I felt successful.

Why the change? While running on the St.FX University track one night after a long study session, I thought to myself that no matter what happened academically, I would become the hungriest person in the room. So I did. A part of me died that night, under the moonlight, running on that track. When that part died, it gave birth to something greater. That run birthed the growth mindset and confidence I needed to succeed in my program of studies and within my business.

Running has taught me many amazing lessons, you just need to listen and apply those lessons. Some of you may find these lessons in other ways of movement as well.

By the end of my Junior year, I had made the Dean's list. I remained on the Dean's list the next year, and graduated as a member of the St. Francis Xavier President's Circle of Young Alumni, which recognizes strong student leaders at the university. I was pleasantly surprised and honoured to have been nominated. Afterwards, I re enrolled at St. FX to complete my Bachelor of Education degree, and quickly became a leader and co-president of the university's Education Department. While serving my student colleagues through this role, in addition to being a full time student, I decided that for me it was more important to have a well rounded set of experiences and skills, rather than top marks. So I began volunteering, working part time, and grew my personal training business on the side. Simply put, I began my side hustles. I barely slept, but I knew that the gifted always rise to legendary. If you are hungry enough, you will rise too.

Upon graduating in 2013, I was reading a Maclean's Magazine article which was telling me that only fourteen percent of Americans at this time were getting jobs directly out of university and, of those, only four percent were being offered positions directly in their field. Gratefully, I was among that four percent. I was offered a job in my field in Raleigh, North Carolina directly following my degree. Why? Because I was hungry. I wanted to create jobs, not just fill positions. In this case, I took an existing position early in my career, and would later create another. And another. Never settle for something less than what you work for. Be the four percent.

So, what does it really mean to be the hungriest person in the room? It means that regardless of your circumstances, regardless of your past, regardless of your level of leadership or your level of education in a specific area, you can still position yourself to use your strengths to win at life and to win within your profession.

Simply put - be diligent. Be committed. Be dedicated. Learn every day. Ask the right questions and don't take no for an answer.

Be bold.

Be brave.

Fortune favours these qualities, especially in a world that needs them! Become your biggest fan, your best advocate, and your humblest of friends.

Many companies in the world want *guts over glory*. They want someone who has a deep drive to learn and to grow. This type of person is much more admirable than a college or university grad student who applies for the same job with a 3.2 GPA and no volunteer or directly-related work experience.

Get busy.

Get dirty.

Be hungry.

Be the four percent.

I am often asked what the hardest thing I have done in my life is, and you know my answer? Tree planting. It sucks. It was by far the hardest, most mundane job I have ever done. I lasted twelve days before deciding that it was better to take the money I had earned early, and head to New York for a summer camp position in the Hamptons. Yeah, I was that guy. But that was the best decision I made that year. Other than a first year Chemistry course, this was the only time I had officially quit something in my life. But the boat needed to be burned. My right elbow even bothered me for about six months after that tree planting job. I remember trying to write out my sports lessons for the day in New York, and having to shake out my elbow after each sentence I wrote. It was a pleasant, but painful, affirmation that I had made the right choice for me.

When I sit around the campfire these days and talk about that job, it still amazes me that I had the audacity to do it. I was crazy and ambitious when I was twenty two. Be the same, and watch where it takes you. The lesson here is that you need to be hungry enough to do what is necessary in getting you to your best decade. It may not always be pretty, but it will be necessary. Tree planting was not pretty or fun, but it provided me with some lessons that I can now share with you and with my future children someday. Some of these lessons included:

1. **There is never an excuse for working in poor weather conditions**
2. **If you invest in something, stay in it long enough to get your investment back**
3. **Never compromise your body for the sake of a few dollars**

There is an old adage that states, "If you are the smartest person in the room, you need to find another room to be in." I totally believe this.

In the film *Now You See Me*, one of the opening lines similarly states, "*If you are the best magician in the room, you are in the wrong room.*"

Powerful thought!

You need to always position yourself in your best decade to frequent the room where you *don't* know all the answers. This may sound scary as hell. That is ok. Embrace it with a full appetite and be ready for a second serving if more challenges come your way. Lead without a title and be a team player no matter which team you are on. Be hungry now to be able to serve those who are hungry later in life.

Relationally, if you are looking to find Mrs. or Mr. Right, you need to first become Mr. or Mrs. Right. One way of attracting someone to you, is to become the person you are looking for. If you both start with and live by that mindset you will have absolutely no problem finding Mr. or Mrs. Right in your best decade, I promise you that.

How can you become the hungriest person in the room professionally in your best decade? Let me share with you twenty ways you can enrich your life and become (and remain) the hungriest person in the room.

1. **Always Know Your Room:** For example, are you in the finance, education, sport or education room? Identifying your room is the first place to start. You need to know which room you are in before you can decide to be the hungriest in that room. My recommendation - do not be in more than three different rooms at a time.

2. **Find Your Strengths:** Are you a good leader? Are you someone who works hard? Are you quiet and prefer to be behind the scenes, or do you like being in front of a crowd? Do you excel in one subject area over another? Write out your top five strengths. If you do not know what your strengths are I would suggest reading *Strengths Finder* by Tom Rath. There is a test at the end of his book, which reveals what your top five strengths really are. Powerful stuff to establish your foundation in your best decade.

3. **Shore Up Weaknesses:** For example, if you are a smart student or a well respected leader in your area of work or study, can you take additional courses to make you more well rounded? If you have weaknesses that are in your basement, you don't need to bring them to the second story of your house of strength. In your best decade, simply aim to get them to the main floor. Once there, go back to focusing on your strengths, and

elevate those through the roof of your house. Blow the lids off your capacity jars!

4. **Know and Appreciate People**: Show others love and respect time and time again, and do it from a position of humility. When you do this, they will naturally want to support and build you up in different areas of your life. That is an educational life lesson that no institution will ever be able to provide.

5. **Live With Intention:** I would suggest going back and reflecting on chapter two of this book. Living with intention will produce mastery, and mastery produces great results. Results mean more than adding extra letters to the signature after your name. Get intentional with your networks and emulate their hunger.

6. **Serve:** No one likes a leader who doesn't know how to serve others. Explorer and international climate awareness game changer, Robert Swan, who hiked both the South and North Pole before the age of thirty three, once said, "Leadership is about servanthood." Serve others first and foremost and that will continue to drive you as you become the hungriest person in the room. (*To learn more about Robert Swan's leadership, check out: http://www.2041.com/robert-swan/, and be sure to sign the petition to reduce global carbon emissions while you are there.*)

7. **Be Fully Present**: There is nothing worse than trying to entertain an important conversation with someone who cannot seem to disconnect from their phone. If you want to be hungry, don't let your phone dictate when you are full, or distract you from eating. In fact, I had an important meeting via phone a while back

with the CEO of a medium sized company. The CEO was texting during our conversation and the whole time we were talking about serious directional perspectives to help him avoid closing the doors, his phone continuously buzzed. I could sense he was distracted during our conversation. The funny thing was that he wanted to talk about what his next steps were with his business and how he could focus in on some specific action items to move forward. Hard to remain focused when something is buzzing you back into surface level thinking. Be present, put the phone aside, and focus on the present conversation.

Get yourself to a level of deep thinking without interrupted thoughts. Reduce interrupted thoughts in your best decade.

8. Look the Part: Have you ever had an overweight personal trainer tell you how to train? Have you had an overweight doctor give you medical advice on how to eat healthy? If you have had either, you shouldn't. This may be brash advice, but you need to look the part for people to take you seriously. This will give you the added edge on the competition who may be in the same room as you, and equally as hungry. Wear a nice suit to work. Shine your shoes from time to time. Add lifestyle disciplines to your weeks to get you to a healthy place. Don't show up to a Chicago Cubs baseball game wearing a New York Mets jersey. You know, the basics.

9. **Communicate:** You do not have to be the loudest person in the room to be the hungriest, but you do need to be heard. In fact, there is nothing worse than being in a room with someone who believes that they know

everything, and that the world owes them something. Please don't be that person. People need to know you are hungry, but they do *not* need you to always be loud about it. Perfect example: one time, I was in a meeting with my specialist team at my school in Abu Dhabi. The Vice Principal was spending time talking through concerns in a certain area, and I remained silent even though I had a lot of leadership and expertise in that area. I waited for him to ask me my thoughts near the end of our meeting and when he finally did, I made it rain. We dismissed for the day and got on with life. Be hungry. Show the world how hungry you are. Do this once and be heard, instead of a redundant five times loudly.

10. Be Consistent: *Being* hungry is one thing, but *staying* hungry is another. It would be easy to read this chapter today, and then show up to work tomorrow ready to be the best, but can you maintain this mindset over time? Being the hungriest is a marathon, not a sprint. Get yourself into a position with a positive mindset each day that enables you to bring your best self to your family, your school, or your work. Do this day in and day out. Don't be a weekday warrior; be a lifetime warrior.

Show up.

Be consistent.

11. **Cocoon Yourself:** I recently read a book by Steven Siebold titled *177 Mental Toughness Secrets of the World Class*. Incredible read. His book first introduced me to the term "cocooning" which, to me, essentially means that it is important to surround yourself with

amazing people in order to do amazing things. Go buy it right now if you want another tool for unveiling your best decade. You need to surround yourself with like-minded people who are also the hungriest people in their areas. They challenge norms, create big visions, and execute day in and day out. You know who these people are. Buy them a coffee and learn how they stay the hungriest person in the room. Doing this now will allow you to become a next level leader.

12. Know Your Role: When I was twenty six, I started a new job and had no idea what my role was, despite my title. It was a very unique role that wrote it's own job description depending on the person employed. I had to navigate those waters without a compass or any real guide. I had a professional growth plan, but it was mostly up in the clouds. I wasn't grounded. It is hard to stay hungry when you don't know what table you are supposed to be sitting at, or what meals you need to prepare for. After six months or so, I began to unveil my role within the organization and adjusted my growth plan accordingly. It helped me become successful and set me on the path to being hungry with a hearty book of recipes.

13. **Rotate the Crops:** Every good farmer knows that you must rotate crops to get a high percentage yield of your product. It is basic science. Harvest half of your crop one year, and half another. Skip a year, then add in a new type of crop to keep the soil rich with nutrients for continued growth. The same holds true for people. If you want to become (and stay) the hungriest person in the room, it is important to find that balanced rotation. Stephen Covey also writes a whole chapter on this in

his book titled, *7 Habits of Highly Effective People*, which I recommend you read or re-read after my book. So, how do we apply a crop rotation mentality to our lives? Try playing a seasonal sport or taking a seasonal holiday. Take a term off from coaching and/or extra curricular leadership obligations after school or work. Don't enroll your kids in every program imaginable. Either way, finding ways to rotate your own crops will not only keep you fresh, but also keep you the hungriest person in the room.

14. Journal: Journaling helps you stay clear in regards to your goals. Recall important daily events that probe you to think critically about where you are, how you got there, and what is ahead for you. Writing and reflecting will keep you hungry.

15. **Focus**: As Coach Taylor from *Friday Night Lights* would say to his team, "*Clear Eyes. Full Hearts. Can't Lose!*" A powerful statement that is all about focus. Focus is dynamic and can produce amazing results if you can master it's amazing ability to push you further than you thought you could go. Right now, I am in the middle of the mall writing this book during prayer time over the PA system in the UAE with about fifty people per minute going up and down the escalator beside me. Oh! And I am also listening to a masterful Irish song called, "The Blood of Cu Chuclainn" on iTunes. Yet, I am so focused on writing that I am not bothered by all the distractions. Why? Because I have trained myself to become *hyper focused. I was able to do this* by reading many of John C. Maxwell's work on supreme focus, and by removing distractions I have better control over my writing space. Focus keeps you hungry. Focus keeps

you determined. Focus will yield amazing results over time in your best decade.

16. Translate: Being the hungriest in one area is not enough. You need to be the hungriest in at least two areas of your life, depending on what chapter of life you are in, and what your priorities are. If you are a student, vow to be the hungriest student in each of your classes. If you are completing an internship, become the hungriest intern the business has ever had. If you are with your family, lead your family well. You set the bar of your life and of your family. Raise the bar high and be the hungriest mother, father, son, or daughter in your family. It will elevate everyone's game and outlook on life.

17. **Start Where You Are:** If you have nothing, that is fine. Some of the hungriest people in the world started with hardly anything and hardly an idea of where they could potentially end up. Successful NBA Owner and Philanthropist Mark Cuban is a prime example. Mark started with very little and had humble beginnings. He knew where he was starting from, but did not shy away from becoming an entrepreneur for the world! In middle school, to increase school spirit, he designed and sold school-themed shoelaces for students. Voila. Instant entrepreneur. He recognized a gap and he pounced on the opportunity. Now he is one of the most successful owners in the NBA.

    Steve Jobs and Steve Wozniak started making Apple products in Steve's garage. Now, Apple is worth more than some countries' entire GDP.

Mike Babcock, Stanley Cup Champion and Team Canada Olympic Gold Medal Hockey coach, was paid very little at the beginning of his career. In fact, in his thirties he almost lost his first coaching job due to athletic program cuts at the university where he was working. As of 2017, he is now the highest paid NHL Coach in history with the Toronto Maple Leafs. A brilliant man who has always remained hungry. You need to read his book titled, *Leave No Doubt*. It will blow your mind.

18. Get Physical: There isn't a hungry person I know out there who doesn't understand the importance of staying healthy through making physical activity and movement key habits within their life. Author Charles Duhigg talks a lot about the important habit of exercise in his book titled, *The Power of Habit*. I cannot emphasize this enough. If you want to get hungry, and stay the hungriest in the room, you need to be moving every day. Movement increases blood flow to the brain and can give birth to creative thinking. I encourage you to read *SPARK*, by Dr. John Ratey for more science behind this research. Being the hungriest means being cutting edge, and being cutting edge means being physical. Being physical means you have balance in your life and it means you are able to handle more stress and outlive those in the room who are hungry but not healthy. I particularly love the following quote from actor Will Smith, which I feel sums this point up nicely.

> *"The only thing that I see that is distinctly different about me is I'm not afraid to die on a treadmill. I will not be out-worked, period. You might have more talent than me, you might be smarter than me, you might be sexier than me, you might be all of those things. But if we get on the treadmill together, there's two things: You're getting off first, or I'm going to die."*
>
> —Will Smith

19. **Evaluate:** When you become the hungriest person in the room, you will experience times when you feel you may be losing your edge. I am guilty of this myself, both in my relationship and in my professional life. So how do I combat this? I took some great advice by John C. Maxwell and I created a spreadsheet (*as discussed in an earlier chapter*) of all my successes; both small and large. If it's a win, it's in the spreadsheet. My spreadsheet is organized into different categories that allow me to constantly reflect and evaluate those areas. Every time I feel I am losing my edge or not gaining ground towards my goals, I get reassurance from my spreadsheets that I am moving in the right direction and that I am creating the life I want for my family and for my career. Look at it from time to time when you need it, then get back to work! It is a life-changing practice that keeps me hungry; you may find it will do the same for you.

20. **Perspective:** When I was pursuing my education degree, I had the honour to be able to attend a

Leadership Conference called the "SLC" or, "Student Leadership Conference". One of the mentors there named Gordon Oliver said to me, "*Learn from the past. Plan for the future. Live in the present.*" It was the most insightful statement I heard that year, which, when said aloud, reminds me of how important perspective is. It still resonates with me today. Thank you, Gord!

When you become the hungriest person in the room, you need to know where you stand in the pack of wolves. You need perspective to know where you came from (*and to remember your roots*). You need to know where you are presently, and you need to know what the future holds for you as you continue to be the hungriest person in the room. A great way to do this is to go back through old journals. Reading your thoughts, ideas, and goals from years back and reflecting on them in your current life is a tremendous way to see growth, while also being provided with perspective.

Perspective breeds confidence.

Confidence breeds action.

Action breeds results.

Results breed added hunger.

I absolutely love this quote from Loretta Claiborne, whom I heard speak at a conference in Abu Dhabi in 2017. She said, "*If I can't win, let me be brave in the attempt.*"

Beautiful.

Admirable.

She is an influential leader in sport, and the day I attended her session she was by far the hungriest person in that room. I was humbled by her ability to translate passion into action to those who were in the same room as her.

If you have other strategies that help you stay the hungriest person in the room, in addition to the twenty above that I shared with you, I would love to hear them and feature you in one of my Medium publications. Email me at faheyconsulting@gmail.com and we can discuss this in deeper detail together. I want to learn from you! In the meantime, continue to build your best decade by staying hungry!

CHAPTER 12
Got It? Give it!

"The best investment you can make is in yourself. The second best investment you can make is through investing in others."

FIRST OFF, WELL done! You have unlocked ten chapters designed to help you begin living your best decade. It may not be perfect. It may not be a linear path to your success and accomplishments. It may be filled with a mixture of successes and failures along the way, but you now have the toolbox you need to help you unlock your best decade. The keys for the toolbox lie inside of you! Whichever decade you find yourself in, I hope this book will help you in some way to live your best decade.

Some days, you will feel that you are spinning your wheels. Other days, you will feel that you are on top of the world. Both are amazing elements to navigate on the journey of life.

Your job is simple. Put into action the things you have learned, unveiled, and excavated through this book. Once you have done this, pass it on to others.

Why?

Because ***the single best investment you can make in life is investing in yourself. The second best investment you can make is by investing in others.***

You bought this book, read it, and have therefore invested in yourself. Now, you need to pass this information on to someone else. If you are living the good life and unlocking the keys to your success in your best decade, yet remain alone in this process, how fun and fulfilling is that? Leadership is not a solo event. Evangelize to connect with others!

You need to have people beside you and around you to share this information with. Investing in others will help you continue living abundantly in your best decade.

I challenge you to find a friend, seek a mentor, encourage a family member, or speak to a stranger about this book. If the world is going to raise the bar for the next decade of leaders, we need the world learning how to live out their best decade. For a lake to feel the ripple of a raindrop, a drop of rain must first fall from the sky. Be that first drop. Make the difference in others by sharing the lessons you learned within these pages.

If you are in school, I encourage you to read this book each year until you graduate.

If you are in your twenties or thirties, the best thing you can do is take a ridiculous amount of notes and scribble all through this book at least once, then lend it to a friend or family member to do the same. Make sure to get it back so that you can capitalize on your notes (*and theirs*) to continue to ***create the best decade of your life.*** Far too often I lend books out with important notes inside, and never get them back. Don't make that mistake! Hold a friend accountable for becoming the best version of themselves and give them a deadline to read the book. Be the best friend you can be and help them unlock their best decade. If you got quality information from my book, give it for free to others!

Also, take time in your best decade to explore life and to gain valuable experiences. I could write a whole book on this topic alone, but many great authors such as Seymour Schulich, have already written incredible books to help expand on this idea. Don't worry about money, or a lack of it, in your best decade. You will sometimes feel like Fred Flintstone as you spin your legs faster than your vehicle is moving, but if you continue to read books like this one you will possess wealth in many forms of currency that can't be easily replicated by others. Your diligence will pay off.

In the back of this book, I have listed my top ten favorite books to help you continue to live out your best decade. The journey starts here and, if you are willing to truly reach your full potential, it won't end until the day you die.

If you are in your forties or fifties, the best thing you can do is put this book on your desk at work or on your coffee table at your house. Answer questions your significant other (and/or kids) may have based on what you have read.

Lead by example.

Live with intention.

Talk with others about specific pieces of the book. Enlighten your colleagues about what you discovered about yourself. Make it a conversation starter. Use some quotes from it to start your next staff meeting. Do what you can to infuse the learnings here into everyday life, especially within your day-to-day work.

As a matter of fact, for each picture I see of this book on a desk at a workplace (*yes, it can be an ebook on your tablet as well*), I will feature your photo on my blog and Facebook page for others to see that you are living out your best decade. I want you to live your best life and to invite others to do the same. The world can improve that much quicker through common knowledge, mobilization, and sharing.

I want to leave you with my ultimate vision for life, and the reason why I wrote this book. I want to add value to each person who reads this and to see the lives of others improve. My ultimate vision is to help you improve your life by diving deeper and discovering your own best decade.

Let me join you on this journey.

Commit to a life of legendary.

Now the real work begins. Using this book as your guide, while also investing in some of the books on my recommendation list, it is time for you to unveil your best decade. From here, I encourage you to continue the conversation with me by connecting with me on Twitter @wellnessrf or Instagram @wellnessrf88 using #**YourBestDecade**.

Just as a plane needs the proper amount of lift and thrust to take off, we also require the same forces in our own lives. My hope for you is that this book serves as a combination of both lift and thrust to help *you* take off and begin the journey through *your* best decade.

I look forward to you telling me all about **#YourBestDecade** along the way!

APPENDIX
My Top Ten Book Recommendations

1. *The Power of Habit* - Charles Duhigg
2. *The 7 Habits of Highly Effective People* - Stephen Covey
3. *Tribe of Mentors* - Timothy Ferriss
4. *The 4-Hour Workweek* - Timothy Ferriss
5. *Leave No Doubt* - Mike Babcock
6. *Strengths Finder* - Tom Rath
7. *The Greatest Guide* - Robin Sharma
8. *Sometimes You Win, Sometimes You Learn* - John C. Maxwell
9. *Crush It* - Gary Vaynerchuk
10. *The Champion's Mindset* - Dr. Jim Afremow

My Top Five Personal Growth Writers

Benjamin Hardy - https://benjaminhardy.com
Nicolas Cole -http://www.nicolascole.com
Tony Robbins - https://www.tonyrobbins.com
Timothy Ferriss - https://tim.blog
Robin Sharma - https://www.robinsharma.com

Made in the USA
Lexington, KY
21 June 2019